The Traveler
and the
End of Time
The secret life of Ken Page

The Traveler Series

Ken Page   Dr. Simon Peter Hemingway

Clear Light Arts - Texas USA

The Traveler and the End of Time

Edited by Mary Darragh Page

Graphic design and electronic production by Alan Klemp

First Published in 1996 by:
    Clear Light Arts
    901B Hwy 80, Suite 222
    San Marcos, Texas 78666-8115   USA
    Ph/Fax: (512) 376-3336

ISBN: 0-9649703-1-7

Forward by Ken Page

In February of 1993, I began to share my stories in a workshop I was conducting in Chapel Hill, North Carolina. I did so, first because I was asked, and second, because I was presenting a new body of material concerning the importance of moving out of polarity consciousness. Previously, I had used my life experiences as examples during private sessions, when it became apparent that many of my clients had sailed the same troubled waters as I. I decided to write this book for the same reason. I realized that my life and my path, if I was able to document it and relate what I had learned, could save a lot of emotional wear and tear on others. It could also assist in providing understanding for what may be happening during this time of accelerated transition and change. These stories were also written so that my children, Ken, Amy, Tara, Kendra, Paris and Sanonda, and grandchildren, Tyler and Emily would understand a part of me and my life and would have the choice to explore other paths.

There are experiences in this book that I am not proud of. Many of the stories that follow reflect the hardship and pain that I either inflicted on myself or others in the name of some self-righteous belief in the victim/savior mentality. As a child, I had always dreamed of being a hero.

I now know that I created all my experiences in the name of a fantasy that was fabricated in my own mind. The hero inside me was for me alone. I have found that my old ideas and beliefs limited my creativity and I could only imagine within their confines. If I continued to hold onto these old ideas and beliefs, I saw that I would keep recreating the same patterns over and over. I finally learned to let go and trust myself. There are no victims, only creators.

In realizing that I am a responsible creator, owning and recognizing my creations, I found quietness in a world of pandemonium, timelessness in a world of chaos, and peace in a world where strife is running rampant. Maybe by sharing my stories, it will help me to ease my own disappointments, and my regrets concerning the painful situations that I have caused. I have played hard—I have left my energetic signature along the way for others to follow. I believe my stories can provide valuable guidance through the maze of emotions, sensations, physicality, and experiences, that we call life on earth. That's why I'm here. That's why I've come to this place. I'm a traveler, and this is my legacy to you.

Preface
by Simon Peter Hemingway

This book is the result of many hours of interviews with Ken Page, archival materials, my own experiences as a student-practitioner of MCH™, and the divine flow of the universe. This project was first initiated by Shirley Holly, who contributed several drafts before retiring to pursue the writing of her own life. Although this work is original to Ken and I, Shirley's hard work contributed to its final shape and form.

Shortly after I began work on this project, I realized that its success was ultimately dependent on Ken's willingness to completely bare his soul in our interviews, for his emotional life quickly became the book's structuring narrative. In this sense, Ken was a biographer's dream come true. He never once protested or answered evasively, even when I asked him the most personal of questions. I watched his eyes fill with tears many times as I queried him repeatedly about the various losses in his past, and those tears set the standard of honesty that I strove to adhere to in writing the story of his life.

Ken was also unstinting in his willingness to allow me to write about times and events in his life that many of us who have had similar experiences would prefer to have forgotten. Although he confessed to a feeling of wanting to close his eyes as he read certain parts of this book, he never once complained to me or asked me to censor any detail. In fact, his only concerns were with the fairness with which the other people in his life were portrayed. The quote from John Fire Lame Deer that prefaces this book is directed toward those readers who believe that their healers should be something other than completely human.

Both Ken and I felt as I was writing the book that we were part of an exciting and unique process, which I hope you as reader will share in. This is as much your story as it is Ken's. We are all each other, after all.

I would like to thank all of my friends at Book People here in Austin, the finest bookstore I have ever been in, for all of their invaluable help and assistance, particularly the staff, past and present, of their Coffeehouse, where I spent two months writing this book. I would also like to thank Sandy Saunders, Daniel Rogers, Mary Page, Shirley Holly, Dianne Cooper and Caron and Geoffrey Cash as well as all of the other readers who volunteered to read the first draft and offered their suggestions for revisions. As always, I have Jeri Moses to thank for offering me constant encouragement and irrefutable proof of the existence of angels.

I would enjoy hearing from readers of this book, and am always interested in new writing ventures. Please contact me in care of the Institute for MCH™ if you have something that you wish to share with me.

Austin, Texas, 1996

The Traveler

and the

End of Time

The secret life of Ken Page

The Traveler Series

Ken Page   Dr. Simon Peter Hemingway

A medicine man shouldn't be a saint. He should experience and feel all the ups and downs, the despair and joy, the magic and the reality, the courage and the fear, of his people. He should be able to sink as low as a bug, or soar as high as an eagle. Unless he can experience both, he is no good as a medicine man.

—John Fire Lame Deer

Near Death

I stared down the telescopic site of the rifle. It was still muggy at four in the morning; I was nervous, and stinging droplets of sweat kept fouling my vision. The black tarpaper under my knees was warm, verging on hot, and I could smell the faint sour reek from the rooftop drain vents. In front of me was a kind of narrow alleyway between houses that opened onto the most vulnerable side of the wood-framed building beneath me. The back of the building, which sat out on piers over the lake, I wasn't worried about. The police car in the parking lot and my employee lying in the bed of his pickup could take care of the rest.

I lowered the rifle to swipe at my forehead with my shirt sleeve. Maybe it was my imagination. Maybe I hadn't heard anything after all. I rested my aching arms on my knees, hoping that my family was asleep. Even my wife didn't know what I was really doing. Almost every relative I had in the world was checked into the hotel below me. My hotel. They thought I was worried about a weather disaster. That's how I had explained the boarded-up windows to everyone when they showed up for the family reunion. What I was really worried about was someone stepping around the corner of the building in front of me with a match, and a glass bottle with a gas-soaked tampon taped to the side. All they would have to do is run forward a few steps, light the firebomb, and then throw a pass that even the worst armchair quarterback in the world couldn't miss. I calculated that I'd have at the most three seconds in which to drop them with a bullet. If I hesitated, or missed, they'd have time to hurl the bottle under the hotel's pier and beam foundation, and I would be sitting on top of a five alarm inferno with my entire family inside.

The problems with bikers had begun almost on the day that I bought the hotel and had steadily compounded, like interest on a bad debt. I didn't have many rules, but the few rules that I had to insist on, like banning knives or gang colors inside the bar, infuriated them. Finally they became enough of a nuisance that the police chief had no choice but to run them out of town. The police chief had called to tell me the bikers had promised to burn my resort to the ground on their way out.

A lone cricket chirped forlornly in the darkness. I thought I saw a bat rip through the cloud of moths around a floodlight like an airborne knife. Then I heard it again. This time it was unmistakable. Someone in boots was walking directly toward me. I raised the rifle, steadying my elbows against the roof's raised parapet, and pressed my eye once again against the sight. It felt like my blood had been replaced with a mixture of pure adrenaline and rage. My finger started the slow squeeze of the trigger that they had taught us in the army. I was primed and ready to kill. I was ready to commit "justifiable homicide."

The footsteps grew nearer. "Burn my bar?!" I wanted to scream, "kill my family?!" I'd show them. I'd teach them a lesson they'd never forget. By now I could hear the crisp sound of gravel crunching under foot. The arrogant bastard wasn't even trying to be quiet. I pressed the rifle stock deep into my shoulder, trying to stop the gun from shaking. I felt like I could almost hear him breathing. The footsteps were so near now that I knew he would be stepping out from behind the nearest house in just a few seconds. I had to be ready. I had to be ready. Then the footsteps suddenly stopped. In my mind I could picture the glow of the lighter as he held it to the side of the molotov cocktail he was going to use to kill my family. I felt something harden within me. All time stopped. I knew that I would kill. A moment later I heard the solid whack of a screen door slamming shut. All of the air went out of me as I folded up over the borrowed rifle like a mother over a dead child. "My God," I whispered, rocking back and forth. "My God." My eyes stung but no tears came. "My God," I whispered again. A blurred rectangle of light winked on and off on the second floor of the building across from me. That was Shane's room. Shane was my neighbor's teenaged son. He came into my bar all the time to buy sodas. I'd nearly killed him.

A single tear fell from my eye to the warm black tarpaper, darkening it momentarily before it evaporated and was borne away by the breeze. An uncompromising hatred rose up like a snake within me, a hatred of myself, my life, and all of my wretched possessions. I wanted to reduce everything I had to the size of a stone and throw it into the sea. I had followed my father's advice to the letter and worked longer and harder than anyone else to become a millionaire. Yet something had never felt quite right. Now, for one brief shining moment, God had parted the curtains to show me what I was really worth. The building beneath me felt monstrous and alien. I would have torched it myself to learn what I had learned that night. Nothing I had was worth killing for. Nothing I had was worth dying for. Nothing I had was worth anything at all.

I pushed the gun away and collapsed backward. A patch of stars wheeled through the clouds overhead. I felt the roughness of the roof against my palms. The sound of blood pounding in my ears slowly gave way to the lake's gentle lapping at the dock. I made many vows that night. I would end up breaking most of them, again and again, until the time when I myself was finally broken.

∞ 2 ∞

Millionaire

The hardest working men that I have ever known were my father and my stepfather. Knowing only their example, I was fated to become a workaholic myself. My earliest recollections of this pattern in my life date back to the time when I was seven. Back then, my stepfather was a plant foreman in a bed factory, and a square-dance caller at night. My mother worked with him at the square-dances collecting money and teaching round-dancing. I shouldered my share of the load by looking after my younger brother and sister until my parents came home, usually well after the three of us had put ourselves to bed. Already, I was learning the responsibilities of an adult, and the loneliness that came with it.

My stepfather's factory made steel bed frames. The frames were held together with metal clamps. Each of the metal clamps was fastened with a single screw that was flattened at the top so that anyone could put their own bed together without tools. The bed factory however, had a problem. Too many loose screws were falling out of the shipping cartons, and the cost of mailing new ones was giving someone in the comptroller's office a headache.

My stepfather decided that someone needed to put the screws in the clamps before the bed was shipped. I eagerly volunteered for the job after my dad told me that I would make $2.50 for each 500 clamps that I assembled, a king's ransom for a seven year old in the 1950's. Each day he brought the parts home from the plant after work. And each day, after I came home from school, I'd dump the screws and the clamps out on the garage floor and work until dinner time putting them together. Later that night, the taillights of my parents' car would recede away down the driveway, headed for the dance hall, and I would spend the rest of the evening supervising my two younger siblings.

After just a few months of assembling clamps for the bed factory, I'd earned enough to buy a new tether ball and a small Dough-Boy swimming pool. The new toys were exciting but equally exciting was the mantle of authority that came with supervising the workers that I had hired to pour cement for the tether ball pole. A seed had been planted within me. I could see right away that there was a clear relationship between how hard I worked and how much money I made. The longer that I stayed out in the garage, the more money I put in the bank. Work harder, make more money quickly became Page's First Law of Accumulation.

Page's Second Law was equally to the point: More money meant more toys. More toys meant more happiness. Any seven year old could have figured that one out. I was a happy guy and before long I had more toys than any of the other kids on my block. I even bought myself a new television, and I knew families that didn't have a television at all. My friends wished aloud, prayed, and sat on the lap of some retired eccentric at the mall for their toys: When I wanted something I divided the cost by my fee per clamp, set my quota, and got cracking.

I never thought too much then about what happened to my old toys once I got tired of playing with them, or about how long they were really capable of satisfying me before I set my sights on buying something else. I just kept on working.

Seven years after I stopped putting clamps together in the garage, I had a summer job working nights at another company my dad helped to run, called General Cable. I was 18 years old. During the day, I was a student at the California College of Arts and Crafts in Oakland, California. I did the usual things that college students did at companies like General Cable, mainly working at different stations on the plant floor, filling in for people on vacation and so on. The plant's buildings were 60 years old, dimly lit, and poorly ventilated—a stark contrast to my environment at the college. Most of the men I worked with had never even finished high school, and I worked under an assumed name for fear of them learning my connection to my father, the plant superintendent.

My dad had told me that if you work two hours longer than anybody else, you'll know more than they will and you'll get ahead. It seemed reasonable and it worked. In fact it worked so well that I would write it into my book of laws as Page's Third Law of Accumulation. That summer I asked a lot of questions, worked extra hours whenever I could, and generally kept my eyes open. By the time summer was over I had a full-time night job at the plant and I was still attending college during the day. By then, I thought I knew an awful lot about the cable business, at least enough to sit down and write a report about the division I worked in. Unfortunately, I didn't have time to wait to hear what they thought about my report in the office. I'd heard my classmates at the college talking about running away to Canada. The Vietnam quagmire was spreading and college deferments were about to become a thing of the past. For the first time in my life, I

15

heard a voice in my head telling me exactly what to do. I stood up, walked out of class, and went straight to the National Guard Armory where I signed up for a 6 year hitch. Only half a year later the National Guard and Reserves were no longer options for anyone, and college students were going to war.

By that time I was already back at General Cable, only instead of pushing a forklift on the manufacturing floor I was upstairs, pushing a desk. The report that I had written caused enough of a stir in the office to get me a new job in management. It wasn't that I was a genius: There were other people that I had worked with on the floor that knew more than I did about the cable business. What made me different was my belief in myself. I thought I could change things and that what I knew was worth sharing. I had energy, ambition, and I liked to work hard. The people upstairs liked that. I know they still do.

General Cable and I finally parted ways five years later when they asked me to go to Memphis to manage a plant that had just been segregated. I didn't make a big deal about it, even though I felt like they were asking me to manage a prison. I had already played quarterback when the company had finally decided to meet its affirmative action quotas, and I was tired of carrying the ball. Carrying the ball meant making apologies for policies and attitudes that I didn't believe in. Having been in the National Guard during the rash of arrests at People's Park in Berkeley had taught me the importance of living my own truth, instead of someone else's. I left the cable company to join forces with my parents, who needed my help with their travel business because of my stepfather's recent stroke. I had already achieved my goal at the cable company, which was to become a plant superintendent just like my father. At 25, I was the youngest one in the company's history. After seven years in the cable business, and 14 promotions, I was restless and ready for something different.

By then I had also experienced my first divorce. I had only liked my wife Linda when we married and expected love was something that would arrive later. Our first child, my son Kenny, was born with a life-threatening birth defect that would require three surgeries over three years to finally correct. Soon I was working seventy hours a week, and traveling constantly to other manufacturing plants that the company had charged me with reorganizing. We had two children by then—the youngest was Amy, and my wife had been complaining about the amount of time that I was away. I left the cable company, expecting that my having more time would be the key to resolving the growing differences between Linda and I. When this turned out not to be the case, I decided upon divorce.

I had been willing to marry someone that I only liked instead of loved, because of the other marriages I had seen and because my previous attempt at marrying someone I truly loved had gone sadly awry. Margaret, my first love, and I had met in high school and fallen hard for each other. Only a year after we graduated, we decided to be married. Two days before the ceremony, everything fell apart.

Margaret still lived at her mother's, which is where she told me she would be that evening, putting the finishing touches on her wedding dress. We had already found and furnished the apartment that we were going to live in after our honeymoon. I phoned Margaret during one of my breaks—I was working a swing shift at the cable company, and her mother answered telling me her daughter wasn't at home. I tried several more times. Soon her mother was as worried as I was. At midnight when my shift ended, I drove home full of foreboding. I tried to put my worries out of my head, but it was hopeless. At 1:30 a.m. I tumbled out of bed, put my clothes on, and ran to my car. I had to wipe my palms on my pants at every stop light. I shook my head to try to clear it. I moved in perceptible increments, like a weapon. I couldn't deny what my body was telling me. Something was terribly wrong.

All of Margaret's windows were dark when I pulled up. I saw an unfamiliar car parked just up the street, on a gentle rise just beyond where you might see it from the house. Not wanting to disturb anyone, I climbed up on a fence and hauled myself up to the second story roof, and knocked frantically on Margaret's window. A few moments later a light came on. Margaret's mother hadn't been able to sleep either. She opened the window for me. I stood staring at the neatly made bed. Plainly, Margaret had not been home that evening.

My head swam with the kinds of terrible images shown in driving classes, as I thought of what might have happened to the woman I had planned to marry. Her mother and I talked for a few moments, each of us trying to reassure the other, and then I left. There was nothing further for me to do there, or so I thought.

Then, I saw Margaret as I walked down the steps toward my car. She was only ten yards away. I knew she wasn't happy to see me. She had come from the unfamiliar car that I had seen parked up the street when I pulled up. It slid past on the street behind us like a float in a grotesque parade, its windows still opaque with steam. I stared at Margaret in shock. I could see the muscles in her throat working. "He didn't mean anything," she blurted lamely. "I'm sorry." I didn't say anything. She kept walking towards me. Everything slowed down. I saw my hand snake out to grab Margaret and throw her against the garage door. Her mother ran towards us, screaming and waving her arms. I looked back at Margaret. Seeing in her contorted and twisted face something I had known all along, I turned and walked back to my car. I never saw her again.

That Saturday, the church where I was to be married was empty but for Margaret's maid of honor, who no one had remembered to call. After the priest finally told her that my wedding was a washout, she made her way to my parents' house to find out what happened. Her name was Linda and she was to become my first wife.

Five years and several relationships came and went in the wake of my divorce from Linda. I kept right on working. By then I had my own travel agency. I was also an executive for McDonalds, a promotions director for a regional shopping center, and a consultant to two other companies. I was well on my way to becoming a multi-millionaire.

In accordance with Page's Second Law of Accumulation, I had been trading houses during that same period, and had worked my way up to a huge five bedroom house in the bay area suburb of Pleasanton and a cabin at Lake Tahoe. We had our own tennis court, a pool, a Mercedes and a Corvette in the garage. "We" was me, my second wife, Rhonda, and my little girl, Tara. Rhonda came into my life as a result of one of my jobs as promotions director for a shopping mall. She won the "Maid of Fremont" beauty contest—hands down. She had won many other beauty contests before that, in addition to the hundreds of trophies she had earned in baton twirling contests before retiring from the sport at age 16.

I had a gorgeous wife, a small mansion, and an abundant income. Most people would have looked at my life then and said that it was perfect. I didn't know why but I thought it was too perfect, like the cowboys would say it was too quiet just before the bushes started moving.

I'd catch myself staring out the bathroom window in the mornings as I got ready for work, and wonder what was wrong. It felt like there was a hole inside me, a hole so deep that all of my fancy cars and other toys couldn't come close to filling it. I didn't know what the solution was, only that something needed to change.

In those days, when I thought of change I didn't think about looking inward or changing myself. I thought instead about altering my external reality. I thought about buying new houses, airplanes, and faster cars, and finding new and more interesting ways to make money. The newest and most interesting way that I'd thought of to make money was to get into the resort business.

I'd been doodling on napkins and running ideas past my wife for several months. My plan was to find an older property with dwindling receipts and use my talent for organization to fix it up. I knew about an older resort town in northern California called Clear Lake where they had just the kind of property that I was looking for. After several scouting expeditions I made a real low-ball offer on a place called Oakes Waterfront Park, a combination mobile home park and marina. Even though the bid was only a preliminary to a serious offer, the owners accepted immediately. I was about to get my feet wet in the resort business.

Later that same day, the man I'd worked for for three years at McDonalds, formerly the third-in-command under Ray Kroc, called me into his office. He explained, in a parade of euphemisms, that they were trimming fat, thinning the ranks, to make the company leaner and more competitive, and well, my services would no longer be required.

"Best of luck, Ken," he said, shaking my hand with a far away smile, like he was sending me off with a penknife to assassinate the Ayatollah. Boy, I thought to myself, he had no idea how lucky I really was. I was spared the trouble of resigning.

I went straight home and jubilantly told my wife that we were moving North to Clear Lake. It was all happening so fast. "So," she asked hesitantly, "we're going to sell the house?"

"Consider it done," I announced confidently. I knew I was on a roll. I called someone who had already expressed interest. They bought it that same afternoon. I had completely altered our reality in less than one day. It seemed as though all I had to do was have a dream and it would become real. I would soon learn that it was just as easy for me to create my worst nightmares.

Six months later, I bought another property named Wiseda Resort. Like my first purchase, Wiseda came at a firesale price because it was in rough shape. I also found out after I bought it that every weekend a hundred surly bikers pounding back store-bought beer in the big gravel parking lot. They came with the place like the employees, some of whom had worse histories than the bikers did.

I requested an audience with the bikers' leader. He was about 225 pounds, dressed in greasy denim and leather rags, and sat regally on a spit-shined Harley softail. His dark sunglasses were about as expressive as two camera lenses. Speaking to the two tiny reflections of myself in his sunglasses, I told him about the $3,300 I had to ante up every month for the mortgage. "As long as you're going to be on my property," I reasoned, "why don't you come in out of the sun and drink my beer."

"Okay," he said. That word was the beginning of a long and troubled relationship, one of several in my life that didn't end until one or the other of us left town. In this case, our divorce would became final the night that I spent on the roof of my hotel with a gun and nearly killed a neighbor kid.

By 1985, I owned three lakefront resorts. I had also purchased a Montgomery-Wards catalog store, which came with a small shopping center. My new three story house on Clear Lake presided over the development. At the same time I held down top-level executive partner positions with two companies in the San Francisco Bay area, and I still owned my travel agency in Dublin, California. The resort bars were cash businesses, and the only trips I made to the bank were to put money in. I had more toys than I knew what to do with, including a sail-boat that never left the dock, and a Cessna 150 that sat on the ground for months at a time. I now had three beautiful girls—Tara, Kendra and Paris—and a wife who loved me to distraction. I was still following my father's maxim, working seven days a week, running two companies from Monday to Wednesday, and then working at my resorts Thursday through Sunday. Everything seemed even more perfect than it had when I had lived in Pleasanton, except for one small nagging problem.

Page's second law, the one that described the relation-ship between things and happiness, was breaking down. I had more things than almost anybody I knew but I was restless and bored. I was beginning to suspect that what I thought were laws had only been theories all along.

The loneliest place I knew of was my bar at Wiseda, where I spent evenings working security. It was a cowboy place, with live music seven nights a week, and it did great business. I spent countless evenings in there, looking for answers in my coffee cup, while the crowds of sweaty drunken dancers ebbed and flowed all around me like fish around a shipwreck. The truth that I was searching for was hidden behind the scenery. It didn't look like scenery to me, even though it was my own creation. It looked perfectly real.

One memorable night when I was working security, I caught someone smashing up a picture frame in a hallway. We had some real art on the walls at Wiseda, stuff that I'd bought at auctions as part of a $750,000 dollar renovation. Since I'd bought most of it myself, I took vandalism very personally.

We ended up in a tangle on the floor; I held the vandal down while he cursed a blue streak. To me that was an acceptable outcome. All that I had to do was just keep him pinned there until the cavalry came. Unfortunately, his cavalry got there first. She weighed about 200 pounds, dropped onto my back like a huge rouged buzzard and alternated between yanking my hair out and beating my head like a piñata.

Enough was enough: I reached up, wrapped a handful of her hair around my fist, and pulled. She landed in a drunken, bawling heap in front of me. I staggered to my feet with all of my white hair standing on end just as the guys from security pounded around the corner like a herd of buffalo. None of them wanted to look at me. I didn't blame them. I didn't want to look at myself either. That was the problem.

Suddenly those antiques weren't worth so much to me anymore. I went straight back to my office and changed out of the red security T-shirt that I'd designed myself. I had co-created one of the most vile scenes imaginable, demeaning myself and two other people, solely because of my concern over my "things." I never worked security again.

The first cracks in the foundation of my reality had already begun to appear the year before. In 1984 I had two memorable appointments with a hypnotherapist by the name of Fred Liedecker. After the second appointment, I grew so enamored of Fred's work that I sat in on more than 200 of his sessions. I was beginning to discover that there were many more worlds than the one that I had invested so much time and energy in constructing for myself.

At about the same time I developed an intense interest in crystals. It began with a business meeting at a restaurant called the Nut Tree, located midway between Sacramento and San Francisco. After the meeting I wandered through the restaurant's extensive gift shop. Almost before I knew it I had filled a basket with hundreds of dollars worth of crystals. Then, as I approached the cash register, I found the source of the strange force that had originally pulled me into the store— a huge smoky mountain quartz crystal, so large that I could only pick it up with two hands. It had a phantom pyramid shape inside of it, and seemed to pulsate with a strange energy. I didn't even bother to look at the price: I had to have it. We had a history together, that crystal and I. I had to take it somewhere, and I had no doubt that it felt the same way about me.

Then came a remarkable trip to the Yucatan that same year with my Uncle, Drunvalo Melchizedek, who I'd grown up with in the late fifties in Oakland. Drunvalo had been given very specific instructions by his guides and angels to visit eight different sacred sites in Mexico and Guatemala, and to leave a crystal at each site. The crystals were carefully chosen by Drunvalo and his friend, Katrina Raphael, the author of the book *Crystal Enlightenment*, and each one of the crystals matched the color of a specific human chakra. We had to visit each of the sites—Uxmal, Labna, Kabah, Chichen Itza, Tulum, Kohunlich, Palenque, and

24

Tikal—in order. Each site fell upon the curve of a fibronacci spiral, and Drunvalo had been given instructions to place the crystals within the accuracy of a single atom, if possible. According to Drunvalo's guides, placing every crystal correctly could permanently change the earth's vibration.

Not only were we wildly successful in finding the perfect spots for each one of the crystals, but when we placed the eighth and final crystal at Tikal—representing the crown chakra—something happened to me as well. There, climbing up a pyramid in the midst of a driving rainstorm, I suddenly felt more alive than I had ever felt in my life. I stood on the side of the pyramid, shouting for joy in the pelting rain like a madman. Then the squall passed and I was left staring at my hands.

I could feel energy pouring through them like they'd been charged somehow, like the key on the end of Ben Franklin's kite. When I breathlessly showed them to Drunvalo, he nodded and raised his eyebrows. He had been traveling the world, searching for spiritual knowledge, for nearly as long as I had been a businessman, and had seen many strange and wonderful things. My own journey was just beginning.

I found out what had really happened to my hands when I got back to California. They could heal. All that I had to do was touch people and they changed. I began by working with Fred Liedecker's clients. Word spread quickly. Sometimes, when I arrived at Fred's office I would find people lined up to see me. If I had any doubts as to whether I was now a different person than I had been before my trip, I just had to look at Fred's clients. The way that they looked at me made me feel different, and it was honoring in a way that being a millionaire businessman never was.

The bell tolled once more for the old Ken Page one memorable rain-soaked night on the Silverado trail, the stretch of highway that connects Clear Lake to Napa. It was late, about 11:00 p.m.; I was about thirty miles away from my home and there were very few other cars on the highway. The remainder of the road was arrow-straight, and so I opened it up a little bit to make time. I held two of the crystals that I had bought at the Nut Tree, nestled in the palm of each hand. Somehow it felt better to drive that way. A glint of light sparkled in the drops of water on the windshield. The glint grew larger, separating into two flickering balls of light, and then into two brilliant headlights. They were on my side of the road.

I panicked and stomped down hard on the brake. All four wheels locked up instantly. The oncoming headlights now filled the driver's window as I slid sideways toward them at fifty miles per hour. Everything began to slow down, becoming surreal. I could hear the tires sliding helplessly on the rain-slicked asphalt, and see the blurred orange parking lights between the brilliant flaring headlights of the oncoming car. My heart pounded like a pile driver. The flaring headlights grew steadily larger, until it seemed as though I were sliding into a brilliant white wall. This is it, I thought to myself. This is what it's like to die.

The next thing I knew I was rolling down the road, in my own lane, at about five miles per hour. I glanced in my rear view mirror and saw the red tail lights of the other car shrinking behind two fans of water in the distance. It hadn't even slowed down. What had just happened?

I pulled over on the narrow shoulder. The crystals fell to the floor. My hands were shaking so badly that the ignition key felt like a live minnow between my fingers. I fell back in my seat. Everything was strange and new. I was picking up scents that I had never noticed before. The rain on the roof over my head boomed like thunder. My car felt completely alien, like an UFO.

Somehow, someone or something had reached down and altered my reality, just enough to keep me alive. I had no idea why. Much later, I would come to believe that in the moment when I should have been killed, a higher aspect of myself from another dimension took advantage of that momentary ripple in time to become part of me. All I knew when it was happening was that I felt very different.

Gradually, the reality of who I was becoming, and of the other realms I was beginning to see beyond the physical, started outshining the world that I had lived in so comfortably for more than thirty years. This process was the working of an alarm clock that I had set long before I was born. The problem was, I liked the bed I'd made for myself—my houses, my businesses, my life. I didn't want to get up.

The first shot across my bow came in 1983 when Clear Lake flooded. The last flood in that area had been more than one hundred years ago. Oakes Waterfront Park, which was on a creek which drained from the lake, sustained the most damage. I set out to sandbag the general store, which was awash in eighteen inches of water. After six hours of filling sandbags and pumping out water, little boxes of jello were still floating around the floor of the store, so we changed our focus to salvaging merchandise. The water stayed for six weeks, which was unheard of for flash floods in that part of California. When the waters finally subsided, we dove right into rewiring, patching, and painting the mobile homes which had been on submarine patrol for a month and a half. Although I had sustained considerable losses, I had survived, and I did not vary my course.

Within two years I had covered all of my losses, and my businesses were thriving once more. Financially, everything looked wonderful. I was glad that we had gotten that flood over with. The chances of another flood in a hundred year flood plain were almost non-existent.

When my wife called to tell me that the lake was rising for the second time, I was staying with her mother while I worked at my two businesses in the San Francisco Bay area. I stared out the window, overcome with dread. Two years earlier, the rains had stopped before Cache Creek had overflown its banks and flooded my mobile home park. Now the flooding had already started and the rain showed no signs of relenting.

I turned immediately to prayer. While my mother-in-law watched television downstairs, I kneeled for hours in my room repeating the phrase that had become my mantra, over and over, until the words themselves didn't make sense to me anymore.

Stop raining. Stop raining. Stop raining, God, please make it stop raining. I prayed over and over again. I had never prayed so hard for anything in my life. I could almost feel the muddy water lapping at the footings of the properties that I'd worked so hard to buy, the properties that I'd almost killed for. Stop raining, I implored. Stop raining. I threw every ounce of my intent, every fiber of my being, into those prayers. I almost felt myself washing away.

By the morning of the second day I was begging. I could see the error of my ways, I could see that I was like a madman that had bet everything on the roulette wheel, I could see how I could change and do it all differently, if only it would stop raining. If only it would stop.

On the afternoon of the third day my mother-in-law knocked on my door. I levered myself up on my sore knees and swung the door open. She took a step backwards. I was a sight, but I didn't care.

"What is it?" I demanded wearily. She stared at me. "What is it?" I asked again.

"Ken," she said, "have you looked outside?" I tore open the curtains. Sunlight streamed in. Birds were hopping about amidst pools of water on the back lawn. I whirled to face my mother-in-law.

"How about Clear Lake?" I demanded hoarsely. "Has it stopped in Clear Lake."

Her hand flew to her mouth. "It stopped yesterday," she said.

When I drove back to Clear Lake that weekend the sun was shining. My lakefront house was miraculously still dry, although the concrete retaining wall over the beach had vanished and half of the roof had blown off of my Montgomery-Wards store. The water had crested at less than an inch below my back door. All it would have taken was a weak breeze to turn my house into a fish hatchery. I felt blessed enough to make a few weak jokes about it all before I pulled out to inspect the resorts.

Wiseda, my favorite of the three, had fared the best with only a few thousand dollars worth of wind damage. Oakes Waterfront Park had flooded, but it could have been worse. The general store was underwater, as were twelve of the fifty-three mobile homes that I had taken over and operated as rentals. Worst hit was the last resort that I bought, Lotowana Village. The lake ran right through the main building.

I immediately got to work. The restrooms inside the bar and restaurant were canoe-only but I still had restrooms outside for the mobile home park, which looked like a refugee camp. Some of my tenants were grimly salvaging their belongings in hip waders. Those people, I thought to myself, could use a drink. I installed a noisy gasoline-driven pump, built a false-floor up around the bar with sandbags, and propped the door open. It wasn't long before people were wading in for a beer.

I had sustained around $300,000 in total damages. None of my property was insured. The insurance companies considered all of them high-risk. Insuring Wiseda alone at $42,000 a year would have bankrupted me. All of my disposable income had gone into the initial $750,000 renovations, and the repairs after the first flood.

I immediately applied for state disaster loans, and had every reason to expect that they would be granted. In the meantime, I had several mortgages to pay and a large payroll to meet. It was March, and if we weren't open for business by Memorial Day we'd go all the way under, like Atlantis. I had $75,000 in credit lines at the bank which I exhausted. From there I went into my personal savings, and my credit cards. My father and I worked around the clock, doing most of the repairs ourselves. I was tired all of the time but I didn't mind. The harder I worked, the less I had to feel.

We managed to get the resorts back into operation by Memorial Day weekend and then it was business as usual again. People rented our boats, used our mechanics, and ate at our restaurants. Everything looked fine, although I was so over-extended financially that it wouldn't have taken much more than a late beer delivery to take me out. Almost every penny that the resorts and travel agency were pulling in was going to debt service, and the resorts still urgently needed repairs that I couldn't afford to give them. I was reeling but still on my feet.

Then came the knockout punch. When the floods hit, I was in the midst of a mandatory remodel, spending thousands of dollars to create a new prototype Montgomery-

Wards store. They had been in the catalogue business for one hundred and eight years. In August, I received a registered letter from the head office. They had written to tell me that they were closing every one of their catalogue stores in the United States. It was completely unexpected. Those stores had been an institution for me, my parents, and my grandparents. They might as well have told me that the Catholic Church had gone bankrupt.

Two weeks later we sued for 9 million dollars. I was confident that any jury would find that Montgomery-Wards had defrauded me when they knowingly sold me a store that they were going to close three months later. In suing them I was butting heads with Mobil Oil, their owner. I still had to honor my end of the bargain, which meant that I had to keep the store open through the end of the year. Meanwhile, Montgomery-Wards closed their distribution center in Oakland. There was no way for me to get stock. Customers would order from the catalogues and I'd have to tell them that we couldn't get their item. Any profit that I had from my other businesses was going straight down the Montgomery-Wards toilet. I saw this clearly but I had my eyes on the nine million dollars that I was sure any reasonable jury would give me. An award of nine million dollars would solve all of my problems overnight. I would be back in the black, bruised but still a success. My identity would be intact.

I managed to forestall the reality of my situation until the end of the summer when the boats that normally buzz around Clear Lake like water striders disappeared, and the seasonal visitors who swell the population of Clear Lake by a factor of ten each summer, closed their cottages and went home. The cash flow, which had been barely adequate to meet my obligations, dried up. For the first time in my life, I had to choose which bills I was going to

31

pay each month. I called the state's disaster office over and over but never got any answers. Finally, in December, they called me. I remember it as one of the worst days of my life. My application for $300,000 in disaster loans was declined. They were concerned about the length of time I had been in business, and the slim profit margins that my businesses showed. I explained how I had plowed $750,000 back into the resorts since I bought them and how that made them worth much more than the appraisals, but my appeals fell on deaf ears. I put down the phone and stared off into space. I had no more cards to play. That evening I made the decision to put my businesses into bankruptcy.

My identity began to break down just like my resorts had. I had constructed my identity in the external world, basing my sense of self on my signature on expensive cars, airplanes, and property. When I started to lose my toys, I started to lose who I was.

Losing your identity and dying are very similar experiences. You can die easily or you can die hard. I chose to die hard. The gun enthusiasts had bumper stickers about how they'd give up their weapons only when their cold, dead fingers were pried loose. The unspoken corollary is that the longer you cling to things, the more cold and dead you become. I was desperately holding onto what I had left, and I felt I was dying inside—slowly and painfully.

The physical or material expression of the way that I was feeling internally was bankruptcy. I went from being an independent, proactive businessman to being almost completely reactive and dependent. I should have gotten an honorary law degree for the hundreds of hours I spent in court and with lawyers, burning up more than $300,000 on legal fees so that the bankruptcy system could treat me like a criminal.

I had been doing a pretty good job of convincing myself that everything would somehow be okay until my house was finally foreclosed on. It happened just after I completed my obligation to Montgomery-Wards and closed the store, which with its papered windows and empty shelves seemed to have become a Taj Mahal-sized monument to personal failure. By then the only phone calls I got were from lawyers. All of the people I thought were my friends had vanished. I felt like I wore an invisible brand that labeled me as a societal failure and there was nothing I could do to remove it. Meanwhile, knowing that I was in Chapter 11, a battalion of Mobile Oil and Montgomery Ward's lawyers were using every stall tactic in the book to keep my lawsuit out of court, and in the process, the suit was moved to Philadelphia. The bank took my house away, leaving my family and I with no place to go. My identity as a provider was shattered. I had failed.

Nothing in my prior life experience prepared me for the grim reality of four simultaneous bankruptcies and a major lawsuit. I tried as best I could to protect my wife and children from what I was going through, and the result was that we lived in separate worlds. I had no one to talk to. I spent what little spare time I had sitting alone on the back porch of my soon-to-be repossessed house, watching the wind and the lake and the stars. Even then I still believed that there was some way out, that my ship could still come in and that everything could be as it once was. Of course, my ship never showed: Clear Lake was landlocked.

That back porch had been the stage of one of my great epiphanies. It was there, in 1986, when I first heard the faint sounds of Native American voices. As I strained to listen, I could only make out one phrase, chanted over and over. The phrase was "Blue Lake." I knew that it meant that I was supposed to take my magnificent smoky mountain quartz crystal there. Blue Lake was high in the Sangre de Christo mountains and very sacred to the Taos Indians. I knew about it because my mother had been instrumental in the campaign to win Blue Lake back for the Tribe from the US government. Listening to those voices at Clear Lake would almost cost me my life.

In the meantime, I was still bankrupt and homeless. With the help of family and friends, I loaded up everything we had and we moved to a much smaller home in Livermore, California. An old friend and business partner loaned me the money to make my down payment.

My father had always said that if you work two hours longer than anybody else you will always succeed because you will know more than any of your competitors. His maxim had always worked for me, just like the way I had assembled clamps when I was seven had always worked for me. Then, when I needed more money I just put together more clamps. Now, I was putting together clamps as fast as I could, night and day, and it made no difference. I was bewildered, frightened, and angry.

I lost my stake in my nine million dollar lawsuit when the proceedings dragged on beyond the time allotted me for my business reorganization and the lawsuit became the property of the State of California. Although it had been established that I had lost 2.6 million dollars, the bankruptcy lawyers that I had hired settled for four hundred and fifty thousand dollars, the exact amount required to pay the major creditors. I'd spent tens of thousands of dollars on legal fees so that I could be recompensed for an act of fraud, and it had all come to ruin as a result of a sidebar conference between two teams of disinterested lawyers that I had never even met in a city I had never visited. All that I'd ever wanted was my day in court and now even that had been taken away from me. Everything that I had created, my hopes, dreams and my pain had been reduced to a mere file number by an indifferent legal system.

While I was suing Montgomery-Wards, I came under attack from yet another quarter. Like a scrappy stray dog, the IRS joined the fray and frivolously sued me for thirty thousand dollars, claiming that I had neglected to file necessary paperwork more than seven years previously. If I really hadn't filed the paperwork that they were talking about, they would have closed me down in a month. As soon as it was clear that I would receive nothing from the resolution of my suit against Montgomery-Wards, the IRS lawsuit was downgraded to a lien, and I was subject to a humiliating interview in which I had to prove that I was absolutely financially worthless.

The only sources of income that I had left were an import company and a company that I had started to make holograms. One of my partners in both businesses, a man named Bill, was having some health problems. I could tell from my training and his story that the pain and illness that he was experiencing was a product of something that happened to him when he was a child. I suggested that he go to see my mentor, Fred Liedecker. Fred visited my partner at his house. My partner insisted that his wife see Fred first. Bill watched in horror as his wife became a three-year-old before his eyes, holding tightly to the old Teddy Bear that Fred used for regressions, and sobbing as she remembered an incident from her past. It terrified him. He interrupted the session, angrily insisted that Fred leave, and bolted the door behind him. I shouldn't have been too surprised. It had been my first reaction to hypnotherapy as well.

The next day, Bill called a closed board meeting to demand that I resign from both companies. An old friend on the board tried to dissuade me from leaving. We went to see a lawyer. Bill, it turned out, had very deep pockets. It was a small matter for him to spend a quarter of a million dollars on legal fees to harass a single adversary. Reeling from the effect of the four bankruptcies that I was already dealing with, I tendered my resignation. In my overzealousness to facilitate healing I had destroyed my last hope of financial salvation. It was one of the most expensive lessons I've ever had. I would never again try to help someone without first being asked.

By the end of 1990, the curtain had finally fallen on the play that I had written and starred in for the first forty years of my life. From that point on, I could only stand and watch while all of the scenery and props were taken away to be repainted and reused in someone else's production, until finally I was left standing on a bare stage. Soon the actors and the actresses would leave as well, and I would be just as powerless to stop them. My marriage was in as much trouble as my resorts, and when it foundered it would take my children away from me. It would also spawn another lawsuit.

Eventually I grew tired of being sued and I left California altogether. By then all that was left of my empire was a ten year old motorhome and my American Express gold card.

It was all that I needed.

∞ 3 ∞

Polarities

The late eighties were a very exciting time to learn about hypnotherapy. Practitioners like Bill Baldwin and Edith Fiore were teaching about demons and entity releasement. Raymond Moody and Elizabeth Kubler-Ross were stretching the boundaries in other directions with their writings about near death experiences and past lives. The air was full of miraculous tales of healing.

After I came back from my trip to the Yucatan with my uncle, I continued to sit in on sessions with Fred Liedecker. It was in these sessions that I discovered exactly how my hands had been changed by my trip to Tikal. First of all, I found that I could pass them over Fred's clients like dowsing rods. When I asked the client about areas that felt different to me, they told incredible stories. The stories were the vehicles for their healing. Then, I discovered that simply holding my hands on people could change them.

One of Fred's clients had just been diagnosed with cancer and was scheduled to check into a hospital the following week. After Fred had moved him into an altered state, I simply laid my hands on the client's stomach. I had no intent, no ideas about what I wanted to happen. Whatever power my hands seemed to have was as new and strange to me as to anyone else.

As I held my hands on the man's stomach, something about the size and shape of a golf ball rose though my fingers. It floated slowly upward to hover at about three feet directly above my hands, like a tiny space ship, and glowed dark red. Then it suddenly shot forward like a bullet, straight out through a wall, and disappeared.

I turned slowly to face Fred. "Did you see that?" I asked him. His eyes were as wide as saucers. "Yes," everyone in the room answered simultaneously, in a kind of collective exhalation. We had all stopped breathing. None of us knew what we had just seen, but we had all seen it.

Four days later, my secretary put a call through to me at the printing company. "Is this Ken Page?" a voice asked tentatively on the other end.

"Yes," I answered. "This is Ken Page." The caller paused for a moment.

"I'm the man you worked with at Fred's house the other day. The one who had cancer. I had to call you."

"Well, I appreciate that," I told him. People often wanted to call Fred or me. It was a way of confirming that they had actually had their experience. "How are you doing?" I asked. "Is everything going okay?"

"It's gone," he said.

I waited for a moment, hoping that he'd tell me more. He didn't, and so I asked: "What's gone?"

"The cancer. All of it. I just had my biopsy. The doctors, they were all arguing with each other."

"That's really great," was all that I could think of to say. My mind was racing in a thousand directions. Had I really been a part of this?

"I just wanted to thank you. I called Fred and he said to call you."

"Well," I said clumsily. "You're very welcome."

After I hung up, I leaned back in my plush leather chair and watched the dance of the lights on my telephone, and thought about how difficult it was to talk about miracles in our culture. There wasn't a single person in my office that I could mention my telephone conversation to. Miracles frightened people. Today, I know that miracles are as much a part of life as gravity, rainbows, fire, and rain. The belief that miracles are as rare as four-leafed clovers tips the scales of power away from the beholder. I didn't need a Commission from the Vatican, or a television crew, to come investigate what I had seen and heard with my own eyes and ears. I had learned to trust what I knew to feel true.

Years later, when I was in private practice, I finally learned what that red ball actually was. I was working with a female cancer patient. The hospice had called me to help her with a visualization that would allow her to sleep. Like many terminal patients I had worked with, she was afraid to close her eyes, fearing that she might never wake up. The radiation treatments had left her as pale and insubstantial as the starched white sheets which covered her like a shroud. A flask of morphine at her bedside advertised her constant pain. She had been given two days to live.

Inside her room it was as quiet as a mortuary, a feeling that was reinforced by the countless bouquets of flowers that surrounded her. They smelled like death. Outside the wind was howling around the corners of the house like a wild animal, and angrily spattering rain against the windows.

I had detected a strong energy around my client, and so as was my usual practice then, I began talking to it, using my client as a channel. I asked the energy if it had a name. This is one of the ways I distinguished between energies and entities. Energies tended to have bizarre otherworldly names, while entities of earth origin usually had the kinds of names that you might give your children.

This particular energy had a name that I'd never heard in a session before. It's name was Cancer.

"Have you ever had a body?" I asked.

"NO!" it shot back assertively, speaking at about ten times my client's normal frail whisper. I asked it where it had been before it was with my client.

"I was with Jonathan!" it blustered.

"What happened to Jonathan?" I asked.

"I killed him!" it gloated.

And so it went, like wandering around a graveyard looking at the names on headstones with Jack the Ripper. It yelled out their names triumphantly, as though they were its trophies. Finally, I tired of this macabre tour.

"And how many other times have you entered the life fields of a human being to kill them?" I inquired.

"Thousands!" it proclaimed.

That's when it finally hit me. I wasn't just talking to something that had named itself after an astrological sign. I was really talking to the essence of cancer.

The consciousness of cancer, it proudly told me, encircled the earth like a huge cloud, 33,000 feet above the surface. It created illness the same way that other negative energies created fear. The more cancer it created, the more people feared it and cancer used their fear like a factory used electricity, becoming more and more powerful. This, I realized, was the solution to the mystery of the enigmatic glowing red ball. It was a visible manifestation of the same energy. When it had shot through the wall of Fred's office, years ago, it had probably rejoined that giant energetic cloud hovering over the planet, just like water evaporates to rejoin rain clouds.

Once I started asking the right questions, I found that there were energies associated with all types of diseases. There was a mass consciousness of AIDS, a mass

40

consciousness of bubonic plague, and a mass consciousness of addiction. There were energies of war, of famine,
and of concentration camps. The last of these was one of
the worst things that I have ever had to deal with. They
were so unpleasant that I wanted to have a shower after
every session with them.

The Hindus called these powerful energies Vritties.
These energies could, once they acquired enough potential
energy, manifest physically as earthquakes or other natural
disasters, just as electric potential could manifest
as lightning.

During one memorable session, I had a client describe
being on one of a fleet of spaceships hovering over San
Francisco. The spaceships were there to try to balance an
immense cloud of negative energy that was hovering over
the city. When this energy shifted its vibration, it spilled over
into our world and became the last San Francisco-Oakland
earthquake. Were it not for the space ships, my client told
me, the devastation would have been much worse.

I learned about blocks very soon after I went into
private practice in 1986. Blocks are what clients use to
protect themselves from painful memories. The more traumatic the experience, the more impenetrable the block
that the client would put around it.

At the time, I began my work by leading my clients
through a visualization. They would tell me about colors
that they saw around different parts of their body and any
presences that they felt that were in their space with them.
Some of them even drew pictures for me of the strange
and sometimes completely alien beings from other dimensional levels that were around them. At the same time,
many of my clients reported seeing symbols as well.
Shapes and symbols, I soon realized, were the language of
the unconscious. Languages were specific to cultures and

history, and in no way could encompass thousands, or even dozens of past lives. Later, I would visit my uncle Drunvalo Melchizedek's mystery school and see this abstract idea explicitly demonstrated with a universal symbol found in all ancient cultures, a symbol called the Flower of Life.

If I encountered a block during a session, I simply had the client remember a shape or symbol that they had already given me during the visualization. In every case the symbol took the client around the block, to a time before the traumatic event took place. This allowed us to tiptoe up to the event in a careful measured way, rather than plunging the client right back into the trauma that they'd worked so hard to forget. Unlike every other technique that I knew of, the symbols never failed to work.

Then, once I had the keys that allowed me to access my clients' most painful memories, I found that it was possible for a client to look at an experience without having to feel all of the pain that went along with it. I simply told them to watch what was happening as though they were seeing a movie. For especially terrifying experiences, I told them to see themselves safely held in my arms like a baby, and to just sneak glances at whatever frightened them. This never failed either.

From triumphing over blocks I went on to make great strides in dealing with patterns. Patterns are those aspects of our lives that we tend to recreate over and over again so that we can understand them. While I think most people who have done any amount of counseling work understand how patterns work in the present, or conscious mind, far fewer people know how patterns affect people across the spectrum of all of their lifetimes. I soon found that the patterns which had the most profound affect on my clients' lives inevitably had their origins in the birth process, or in a past life. The patterns that were accessible to their conscious mind were echoes of these more traumatic events, which usually involved violent death. Thus, what I would consider to be the major patterns in someone's life were only amenable to healing techniques based on an awareness of past lives. As long as the original event, which created the pattern, was in another life, a "conventional" therapist wouldn't be able to help the client to understand it and the client would thus continue to recreate it in their present life.

As an example, consider one of my clients who came to see me with a pattern around strangulation. He had been born with the umbilical cord wrapped around his neck, and had nearly fallen victim to several accidental strangulations since that time. The origins of this pattern lay many lifetimes ago, when he was betrayed by someone he loved and unjustly hung as a result. He had not completely processed this event and it still had a major charge to it. All of the accidental strangulations in his present life, and in previous lives, were attempts by the conscious mind to access this event, which was secreted in a locked file cabinet deep in the unconscious, a file cabinet that the conscious mind didn't have a key to.

The difficulty in dealing with patterns like these was in knowing precisely which past life the client needs to access to find the original incident, rather than one of countless repetitions, which overlaid each other like the skins of an onion. Mistaking one of these layers of repetitions for the original experience could not only be costly in terms of money, but it could also eventually cost the client their life.

I found a way to go directly to the very heart of the onion, without having to look at all the layers. There are two aspects to this process, which I call pattern removal. In the first place I realized that the clients always directed their own healing, and that I was only the facilitator. This meant that my clients had to come to me knowing exactly what they wanted to work on. I just needed a way to communicate with the all-knowing librarian within them that knew exactly where to find the book that I needed to open.

The breakthrough came when I realized that the same energetic scanning process that I had begun to develop after my visit to Tikal, could also be used to find patterns in my clients' energetic fields. These patterns were like footprints. Using them as a key, I could access exactly the memory in my clients' unconscious that they had come to work on. They were a way the client's higher self and I were able to communicate directly, in the same way that a person goes to a medical doctor and points to the part of them that hurts. The speed at which this scanning process allowed me to work made me look like a miracle worker. People who came to see me who had seen every other type of therapist I'd ever heard of, and some that I hadn't, were able to get results with me in one session. Before long I was booked solid every weekend.

My clients brought me a wealth of new information. I soon learned to let go of my preconceptions, and once I did there was no limit to what the universe had to offer. For example, during one session I looked up from my client to see three spinning silver pyramids hovering beside us. My jaw dropped. "I'd like to speak to the three silver beings," I finally stuttered. "If those beings could speak to me now, what would they say?"

"We are from another reality," they offered.

"What are you doing here?" I asked them.

"We're curious about you," they replied.

When I made it clear that they were interfering with my client's life, they agreed to leave. Like many beings from other dimensions, they had come to learn more about the human emotional body. I gave them as much information as I could about it before I sent them on their way.

Nobody that I knew of was breaking spells, dealing with the mass consciousnesses of diseases, freeing trapped extraterrestrials, and matching wits with Satan on an almost daily basis. If that wasn't enough to destroy anyone's reality, I don't know what was. Other hypnotherapists stopped at the threshold of past-life regressions because that was the limit to their reality, the theoretical end of their world. I knew what the threshold to their worlds was because I was getting the clients that they refused to see. I still am. Beyond their known world, like the old maps said, lay monsters. I knew all about the monsters too: my clients drew them with crayons for me. That's where I was, with the monsters, and I was more and more afraid that I was about to fall off the edge of the world.

I had no one to compare myself to, no reference points. Beyond the tales of healing and the casting out of unclean spirits in the New Testament, the only established contemporary model I had for what I was doing was the Catholic exorcist, and that was almost worse than no model at all. Exorcists died like flies. It is a documented fact that Catholic exorcists have an average life span of less than 5 years once they begin their work.

The professional isolation that I felt soon spilled over into my personal life. I even stopped talking about my work to my wife, who had loyally studied hypnotherapy with me. I didn't know any way of telling her about the extraterrestrials, the demons, and the ghosts who had become part of my reality. Although I didn't understand it at the time, this impulse to isolate myself was rooted in events of my childhood that had convinced me that I was dangerous. The beings that I talked to threatened me all of the time. My family was defenseless against them—or so I thought, and so I refrained from ever talking about them in their presence.

The real problem was polarities. Polarities were what someone in my line of work would inevitably encounter as long as they believed in a universe of opposites. Believing in a universe of opposites simply meant investing in the difference between light and dark, good and evil, and so on. Investing meant taking sides.

Seeing the universe as made up of division and struggle is a function of a certain type of consciousness; seeing it as oneness is a function of another. We are all making the shift from polarity to unity or Christ consciousness, each of us at our own pace according to divine timing. At the time, I recognized the idea of oneness but I thought of it as a consequence or outcome of all of the battles that I was fighting. The way I saw it, once all of the darkness in the world had been balanced off of the face of the earth, then we would have oneness, not before.

I began to believe in my heart that I was in grave danger and that this danger extended to those around me. I know now that when we create—and we are all creators—from a place of polarity consciousness, we create both good and evil, and if we believe that our creation can kill us, it eventually will. In a sense, Catholic exorcists really kill themselves, and this is the mechanism. In my case, my belief in polarities, and in my role as Lucifer's adversary, would persist not only until I had nearly destroyed myself, but also until I had nearly destroyed everything that I loved.

Because my curiosity about energy was insatiable, I was drawing these lessons to me with increasing frequency, and they kept getting stranger all of the time. I had clients who had been raised inside Satanic cults to be human sacrifices, clients who came to me to have alien implants removed, and clients who came to me to have curses and spells broken.

As I attracted ever more powerful polarities, I began to suffer ever more powerful attacks from my invisible energetic adversaries. They ranged from a scratching or clawing at my face to headaches and pains all over my body that would leave me rolling in agony on the floor. These attacks were the physical manifestations of the belief system that I held when I started my work. The energy that they used against me was the energy that I gave them.

In those days, my encounters with the demonic were decidedly cinematic. The room would fill up with the stench of rotting flesh, the temperature would change, and right away the demonic entity and I would get into an argument. "She's mine!" the client would hiss.

"No, she's not," I would insist firmly. "You no longer have the right to interfere with her life."

"You can't do anything about it!" the client, still channeling the demon, would howl.

"Oh yes I can," I'd assert, and so it would go. The contest of wills would continue to escalate, each of us calling upon our respective legions of helpers until finally, with the aid of the dolphins and whales, the demons were dispatched. Dolphin and whale energy was invaluable in holding energies and entities in place until the appropriate angelic helpers could be summoned to help them find their way home. I'd learned about the dolphins and whales from Bill Baldwin, but I didn't understand why they were so useful until much later when I finally began to understand that there was an alternative to the universe of polarities, a place of balance between them where light was clear instead of white or dark.

Each time I called upon my legions of helpers to match the negative energy that was being directed at me, I created in essence a vacuum, which then allowed more negative energy to flow in. This flood of energy created the striking physical manifestations. As both types of energy were inexhaustible, it was an equation that I could never solve in my favor.

Meanwhile, my marriage was becoming like that famous suspension bridge that they show movies of to physics and engineering students—the one that whips back and forth in the wind like a stick of licorice before it breaks. I had never been a perfect husband. My wife's relationship to the old Ken Page had essentially ended in 1985 on the night when according to all logic I should have been killed by a head-on collision on the Silverado Trail. I was no longer a millionaire, no longer interested in being one, no longer so many things that I had once been. I was confused about reality, see-sawing back and forth between the worlds my clients brought to me and what was left of my business career, no longer certain of what was illusion and what was real, and unable to talk to my wife and family about any of it.

I thought often and obsessively of the accident that nearly took everything that I had left away from me. My wife was driving up to see me on that same stretch of road where I had become someone else. I was in a meeting room at a five-star hotel in San Francisco. My client's pager interrupted our business meeting. He strode quickly back from the pay phones, ashen-faced. "There's been an accident," he said woodenly.

Thirty minutes later, I was in the hospital driveway waiting for the ambulance. I stood behind it as it backed in. The lights inside the ambulance lit it up inside like a horror exhibit in a wax museum. I could see the pale frightened faces of my two daughters. The EMT was bending over my wife, who was strapped helplessly to a backboard, I could see the whites of her eyes as she tried in vain to turn her head to messenger reassurance to our daughters, Tara and Kendra. The ambulance's back-up alarm echoed the urgent warbling of the pager that had summoned me. A white-haired helpless ghost slowly enlarged in the ambulance's rear windows. It stared accusingly at me, its eyes welling with tears. Everything you're close to dies, the face said, recounting my crimes. You're a curse to everything that you love.

The feeling of helplessness stayed with me. My wife had driven into a rock wall at fifty miles an hour. The impact broke her back and snapped one of my daughters' arms. My wife was bending to pick up a lost cassette when it happened. The cassette was the soundtrack to the movie *Stayin' Alive*. She had suddenly had an urge to play it.

I had nearly lost my wife once already. At the time I had almost destroyed our marriage. My wife's response was to almost destroy herself. I reconsidered. She recovered. For a while we were closer than we ever had been before. It was blissful. Then came the flood. After the flood came bankruptcy, and my burgeoning interest in hypnotherapy. Now I was ready to destroy our marriage once again.

The bridge between my wife and I finally broke when I met Melody. Melody was a psychologist with a Ph.D., and she was the first person that I had met who actually knew what I was talking about. I felt like the condemned man who finally meets the lawyer who believes him. Melody knew things that I didn't know, things about witchcraft and the feminine dark side that I was driven to understand. She in turn was fascinated by what I knew, and before long we were seeing clients together. I was soon spending more time with her than I was with my own wife. The inevitable happened. I was convinced then that my family was better off without an exorcist around them, particularly my children. My deep and abiding fear that the forces that I was battling with would come for them led me to recreate the ancient drama of the hero who leaves behind everything he loves to face his destiny. I would find out later that this was an old pattern from a previous lifetime.

My children cried and cried when I told them. "Just stop daddy!" my youngest girl, Paris, kept saying, repeating it over and over like the incantation I had once used to try to make it stop raining.

"Daddy can't stop, sweetheart," I repeated back to her. "Daddy can't stop. Daddy can't."

"Daddy!" she cried, almost hysterical now. "Daddy don't." My tears mingled with hers to darken my shirt sleeve. My other two daughters watched this drama, stricken and mute, from their beds.

"Daddy can't stop," I said again. I knew it in my heart to be true. Daddy couldn't.

I drove back from Livermore that night, and cried most of the way. Every song that played on the radio, every shadow on the side of the road, every scent in the night air, only seemed to whisper to me of my loss. My wife had trusted her life to my certainty when we had all set sail together so many years ago. Now I had no more certainty than a dandelion seed tumbling in the wind. The stars that I had navigated by were constantly shifting. I had first set my course by my father, like any son. He had been the model for everything I had wanted to become. After I made a terrible mistake that irrevocably altered the nature of our relationship, I was compelled to look elsewhere for models of who I was to be, and ultimately I would be forced to look deep within myself.

Eventually I would leave Melody as well. I would make one more attempt to reconcile with Rhonda, but it would fail. We would have another child together, Sanonda. Years later, Rhonda and I would find ourselves embroiled in a lawsuit that would last for years. The judge found my passion for healing to be nonsensical and ordered me to keep working as an executive at the printing company. Together, my wife and I were spending $30,000 a year to prove who was the more righteous, and poisoning ourselves and our children in the process. I decided to stop fighting and leave California for good. When I did, the long drought that had begun five years ago on the second day of my three-day prayer vigil would finally end.

∞ 4 ∞

The Mistake

Even before my bankruptcy, managing my resorts was a real challenge. I was able to buy the resort because the owner had lost his liquor license after his bartender sold heroin to an undercover detective. I found out soon afterwards that I had as much in common with the employees of Wiseda as oil and water, not to mention my customers, many of whom had prison records. I had to fire my janitor after he stood up and urinated on the bar during business hours. Not long afterwards, someone set my truck on fire out in the parking lot. The first time that I brought my wife Rhonda to the bar, to hear the country and western band I had installed there, she sat and sobbed at our table for the entire evening. She couldn't believe that we owned such a terrible place.

I knew I needed some help, someone as tough as nails who I could depend on and trust in any circumstances to help me clean the place up. My biological father fit the bill perfectly. I knew that he had just been laid off from his job as manager at a lumber company in the Northwest, and so I called him. He flew down from Oregon to look at the properties and within a few weeks he had installed himself in a double-wide mobile home at Oakes Waterfront Park. He agreed to manage my properties for me, and his wife would look after the general store next to their home.

My dad loved to work, and tough as he was he had little difficulty earning the respect of even my most hardened employees. They called him "Pappy" and deferred to him because he made it clear that he would tolerate nothing less. At Wiseda he was in his element. When he was younger he used to leap onto bars and proclaim: "I can out-fuck, out-fight and out-drink any man in here." The room would fall silent while he stood up there, arms folded, waiting for a challenge. No one ever said anything. They were scared of him.

My father was also one of the nicest men in the world, so long as he wasn't drinking, and he was a peerless manager. We worked together to change the bar into the kind of place that wouldn't drive a man's wife to tears, as it had mine. This wasn't easy. Some of our employees were frightening new customers away. The worst of all of them was J.R.

J.R. was 6 feet 4 inches, slim, sinewy and as mean as a snake. He'd worked on drilling rigs until a knife fight in a bar cut him up so badly that he lost the strength in one of his hands. The fight happened three years ago, in Wiseda. Soon after I met him, he asked me to guess how many times he had been married. I shrugged my shoulders. "Four?" I guessed, "Five?"

He laughed. "Nine," he said, watching me carefully to gauge my reaction. I did my best to remain expressionless.

"You must pay a lot of alimony," I told him. "How do you handle all of that on what I'm paying you?"

"That's the trouble with your kind," he said, grinning. "Who ever divorces them?"

I stared blankly at him for a long moment. "I never thought of that," I replied, flatly.

J.R. was a major roadblock in our efforts to improve relations with the Clear Lake police department. He played third base on the bar's softball team. The night before we were to play the police department, J.R. got drunk in the bar and announced that any policeman who tried to run past him would have his legs broken.

The police chief called me the next morning. It seemed that everyone in Clear Lake had been present to hear J.R.'s drunken ranting. The game was canceled. Even the police were afraid of J.R. My dad's eyes narrowed when I told him about the phone call. "Great," he said. "Now we can finally fire that bastard."

We had wanted to fire J.R. for a long time, but knew that it we'd have to have a good reason. He was as volatile as gasoline and never went anywhere without a nine-inch knife strapped onto his belt. The police department had provided us with the ideal solution to our dilemma: We could fire J.R. and blame them.

We still thought that J.R. might still try to kill us, and so we staged the night of his firing as carefully as the opening night of a play. While our security guards loitered strategically across from us at the bar, my dad and I sat down with J.R. in one of the bar's scarred, dark wooden booths. We both held cocked .38 caliber revolvers under the table.

J.R.'s face didn't betray anything when we told him that we had to let him go because of what the police chief had told us. My dad and I watched him slide his knife out of its sheath. It was freshly sharpened on both sides and had a blood channel in the center. It gleamed in the light like a polished mirror as he slowly and deliberately picked his teeth with its tip. I could feel my hand shaking under the table. The handle of my revolver was slick with sweat. Both my dad and I knew that we would only have a second or less to react if J.R. decided to attack us. He held our attention like a magician. We didn't dare to even blink. J.R. was deciding whether it was worth his while to kill us.

J.R.'s knife floated downward to rest against his bare forearm. He looked down at it as he began slowly and deliberately shaving the hairs from his wrist to his elbow. Not only was he demonstrating just how sharp and deadly his knife was, but each return stroke of the knife could easily be extended to a lethal jab straight to my heart. The blood channel in the knife's center would allow him to quickly pull the knife out again and go after my dad.

The three of us sat there, not noticing how quiet the bar had become. J.R.'s dark hairs continued to pile up against the knife blade and sift downward like ashes onto the white linen tablecloth. The knife made an evil scraping sound. I could feel my hands turning into two blocks of ice as my body prudently rerouted blood away from my extremities. Finally J.R. looked up and right into my eyes.

"I'm going to kill him," he said. His words hung in the air between us like a bad smell. I wanted to look to my dad for support, but couldn't.

"Kill who?" I inquired, doing everything in my power to keep my voice level and even.

"I'm going to kill the police chief." He nodded as he uttered the words, as though he were agreeing with himself. I let some of the air I'd been holding in my lungs seep out, but didn't yet dare to move my eyes. "I don't blame you guys," he said as he lowered the knife out of view and slipped it back into its leather sheath. My dad and I finally looked at each other. We had been spared.

My father and I had many similar experiences, all in the line of duty. We broke up fights, and evicted drug dealers and prostitutes, like two gunfighters hired to clean up Dodge City. However, things weren't always rosy between us. My dad could either be a maudlin, or a mean drinker. When he was maudlin, he would lapse into talking about how much he loved my mother, often forgetting that his new wife was present. Most of the time he just got squint-eyed and mean. I had to move him out of managing the bars, for his own good.

Then, one day in January 1985, the worst happened. I was reconciling receipts with deposits so that I could pay my taxes. Something was wrong. No matter how many times, or how many ways I tried entering the figures into my calculator, Oakes Waterfront Park came up $15,000 short.

Oakes Waterfront Park was where my father and his wife lived. They ran the resort and no one oversaw them. The deposits were entirely my father's responsibility. Everything seemed to point to him, or to his wife. I felt sick inside, and terribly sad.

My business partner, Rhonda's grandfather, had none of my misgivings. "We have to fire him, Ken," he said. I just looked at him. What I was feeling was beyond words. "And, we have to get our money back," he added firmly.

I told my partner that I would fire my father, but that I would be responsible for the missing money. He nodded, considering this. It was worth it to him to have me do the firing. All he cared about was his investment.

I walked back to my car, feeling as though my body was slowly turning to lead. I had fired hundreds of people as I rose through the ranks at General Cable, but I had never felt like this before.

Two days later, I caught up to my father outside of the general store at Oakes Waterfront Park. "I need to talk to you," I said. My heart felt as cold and lifeless as a stone. My father stood waiting. He looked tired and old .

"There's some money missing from the resort," I told him. "A lot of money." My father kept looking at me. I felt like an insect impaled upon a pin.

"I talked to my partner, Ed." I plunged on, feeling compelled by some kind of terrible momentum, a nameless gravity that was pulling me into a dark, lonely pit. "Dad, I have to let you go."

I had said it. We stood there, father and son, together, but miles apart. I felt the way I had when I was ten and shot my first bird with a BB gun. An invisible chasm had opened between us, a chasm so deep and so wide that it defied description.

My dad smiled sadly. He lifted his arm up and squeezed my shoulders. "I understand your position," he said. I waited for him say something else, to deny my accusations, to say anything to lift the cloud that had descended around us. Instead we stood there awkwardly until he dropped his arm to his side. I couldn't bear it any longer. He had already forgiven me.

"I have to go," I said.

I hurried away to the safety of my car. I glanced up as I drove away. My dad hadn't moved. I watched his figure grow smaller and smaller in my mirror until I couldn't see it anymore. He was sixty three years old.

My dad remained in the mobile home for several more weeks while I ran the businesses without him. Finally, he and his wife moved down to Concord, California to manage an apartment complex. I continued to pore over the books, trying to find out exactly what had happened. There was much more money missing than I had first thought, more money than I thought my dad or his wife could ever possibly steal. About three weeks after my father had moved away for good, I finally understood the scale of mistake that I had made. I sat in my office with my chin in my hands staring at the figures, numb with shock, disbelief and grief. I had been wrong.

The real culprit was the bar manager at Wiseda, a woman named Sandy. When I told her that there was money missing, she said: "Today's my last day. I have to go." She had stolen over $100,000. I felt no joy in telling her that I knew. All that I could think of was my Dad, and what I had done to us.

It would be many years later before my father and I would have some semblance of a normal relationship again. By then all of the resorts were in receivership, and I had almost nothing to my name. I had told him many times how sorry I was, but in the end it never really mattered. I had made a mistake that probably hurt him as much as anything else that had ever happened in his long and difficult life, a mistake that he would carry with him until the day that he died. We knew all of this but it didn't matter. We were tied with blood and bound by love. He was my father and I was his son.

∞ 5 ∞

Polarities Revisited

I sat in a windowless room facing a large mirror. A psychologist sat across a table from me, with a telephone in front of her. I knew that there was a panel of several more psychologists and a video camera in a semi-darkened room on the other side of the mirror. They were my jury. They had convened at my behest to see if I should be committed. I held my head in my hands as I told the psychologist that I thought I was going to die. A light flashed on the phone. She picked it up and listened to it for a moment. Someone on the other side had requested a clarification. "Are you telling me that you're planning on killing yourself?" she asked pointedly.

"No," I sobbed brokenly, "but if I keep on doing what I'm doing I'm going to die. It'll kill me, I know it will." I told her that my wife had sued me, that a judge had ordered me to keep my job but that part of my life was becoming a poison to me, and that if I kept taking the poison I would die. "I can't do it any more," I cried. "I just can't." The doctor was careful not to betray any emotion. The big mirror revealed nothing except for my reflection, a weeping middle-aged man lost in a big white room.

The doctor picked up the phone again and listened. "What do you want from us?" she said.

"I just need to know that it's okay," I said into my hands. "I need to know that it's okay for me to go and be a healer even if the courts, society, my wife, and everyone else says that it's not. I need to know that I'm not the one who's crazy. I need to know that I can do what I love."

The psychologist pursed her lips professionally. "We can't tell you what to do," she said. "Your life is your responsibility."

I shook my head helplessly. "Then I don't know what's going to happen to me. If I keep working at my job I'm going to die. I just need to know that it's okay to do what I love to do."

A speaker crackled into life. Somebody somewhere behind the mirror had thrown a switch. "Mr. Page," it said. I looked up at the stainless steel speaker grill above me. The voice was devoid of all expression.

"Go for it," the disembodied male voice said.

To anyone else that voice would have sounded like the speaker inside a plastic clown's head at a drive-in restaurant but I heard the voice of God, speaking directly to me. I sniffled and wiped at my face with my hands.

"You mean it?" I asked hopefully. The doctor sitting across from me nodded. They meant it. I was okay. Everything was going to be okay. I felt the corners of my mouth lifting into a smile. My eyes still stung but now they stung happily, like the kind of sting you get at the end of a good movie or when you see your child for the first time.

The doctor was speaking into the phone. She covered up the mouthpiece when I looked at her. "Was there anything else?" she asked politely.

"That's it!" I said, practically shouting as I grabbed my jacket. I nodded deferentially toward the big observation mirror. "Thank you," I told it reverently. I bowed slightly as I left, as one would when crossing a temple threshold. My reflection bowed back. Behind it, the unseen doctors sipped stale coffee and spun in their armchairs. One of them filled out a form on a clipboard. Another mental health crisis solved.

The breakdown that brought me to the hospital was occasioned by the end of my marriage, the loss of my children, and a court order requiring me to continue working at a job that I had grown to loathe. I had met Melody, the psychologist who had been the catalyst for my divorce, in 1989, two years prior to my experience in the hospital. Feeling that I had much more in common with Melody than with Rhonda, and that I had become a danger to my family as well as myself, I asked for a divorce. As was my pattern with my first wife, Linda, I had worked as hard as I knew how to give Rhonda what she wanted, even to the point of giving her my house, my furniture, and more than half my income. At that time, I felt that working hard and being the best provider possible were ways of showing love. Understandably, it was never enough. Although I tried to explain it to her many times, Rhonda couldn't fathom how I could put my relationship to God ahead of my relationship to my family. She couldn't even understand my concept of God, which wasn't dependent on anyone else's. Nevertheless, I still loved her, and I didn't want to lose my children. At the same time, my thirst to understand the hidden dimensions of the human soul was more powerful than any other force in my life. My search for knowledge had replaced my addiction to work. I was out of control.

Almost as soon as I left Rhonda, I knew that I had made a terrible mistake. I attempted to reconcile. To this end I moored my motorhome in the driveway of our house in Livermore. A garden hose and an extension cord snaked into the house for water and power. It was a tenuous connection but it was all that my wife would permit me and I was grateful for it. I could spend hours on the weekends playing with my children until she sent all of us off to bed. I don't know what the neighbors thought, but I earnestly believed that I was succeeding in regaining my wife's confidence—until the day when she knocked on the door of my motorhome to bring me the final divorce papers. I told her that I didn't want to sign, that I still loved her.

Rhonda sighed wearily. She'd heard me promise her the earth, sky, and the moon and all she had was this house and by God she was going to keep it. She pushed the thick sheaf of papers across the table. The motorhome's lights flickered as the house air conditioning compressor kicked in. Rhonda folded her arms. I signed the papers. The next weekend she asked me to leave. The reconciliation had been nothing but a fantasy on my part. My signature had been all that she had ever really wanted. The house and the furniture was hers. She deserved it.

I trundled my motorhome and my car back to the house that I'd leased with Melody to find half of the furniture missing. A scrawled note said that she'd taken it in payment for the year of free therapy that she'd given me. I hurriedly dragged the rest of the furniture out to the garage before she could come back for it. I could tell that my neighbors were watching but no one stepped out from behind their drawn curtains to offer to help. I felt like a leper.

When I came back from my job at the printing company the next weekend, the refrigerator was gone. I stood blinking in front of the square patch of bright linoleum where it used to be, holding one hand absently in midair. Melody breezed past in the hallway. She paused to look at me like one of my clients who was channeling Lucifer. A moment later the door slammed. I didn't know where she was going, only that it was well-furnished.

Although I was too deep into the role of victim then to fully understand it, what was happening was that the world of polarities that I'd immersed myself in was becoming physical. The energies that I was drawing to myself as an imagined beacon of righteousness were not only affecting me but everything else around me. The result was that I was finding myself lost in a world of opposites. People either loved me or hated me, admired me or despised me, praised me or vilified me. Mostly it was the latter. The amount of negativity that I'd created around me was staggering.

I tried to go on living with Melody but it was like the siege of Leningrad. We had no refrigerator, no furniture beyond what I'd locked away in the garage, and only space between us where there had been closeness. We ate our meals out, barely talked to each other, and came home only to sleep. I knew what she was angling for: She wanted me to go so she could keep the house. I had some experience with these things. Finally I got tired of eating Chinese food up in my room. I gave up the siege, taking my bedroom furniture with me.

My aunt Mary, who was a partner with me in one of my waterlogged resorts and knew something of my predicament, offered me a position up at the stables that she ran in Oakland. She'd sold the stables to the city but still managed them and owned the tack store. The store did good business. I could eventually take it over, and in the meantime I could work there and look after the horses for her. The money was a tiny fraction of what I was used to being paid but at least I'd have a place to park my motorhome, away from all of the people that had become as angry and disappointed with me as I was with myself.

I had time to look after horses because the heat of the scorn that was being directed toward me had all but evaporated my healing practice. Apart from the people that I occasionally was asked to help die, I had no clients. Rhonda, my ex-wife to be, had made a lot of phone calls that began with the words, "I think there's something that you need to know about Ken." What they needed to know was that I was a monster for leaving her for another woman when she was pregnant with our fourth child. It wasn't that I didn't feel as though I deserved her scorn—I just wasn't so sure about deserving everyone else's.

Rhonda sowed the seeds of her vengeance far and wide, and their bitter fruit ripened to be pecked over and consumed and spread even further afield. Wherever I went the sound of the bell that she and I had hung around my neck preceded me, and it wasn't long before the weight of all of the projections that were being directed my way started to affect the way that I saw myself. Even Melody, the licensed psychologist and freelance furniture repossessor, had caught the revenge bug and had warned our joint clients in her most convincing professional jargon that I was unstable and therefore untrustworthy.

Only the horses would have me.

We fell in love, the horses and I. In the depths of their dark liquid eyes I found the perfect compassion and unconditional love that I had been looking for all of my life. They offered me the best reflection of the parts of myself that no one else seemed to be able to see anymore. Driven to heal, and with no human clients, I nourished that spark within me by becoming a healer of the four-leggeds. They offered me their teachings in return. I learned to look carefully within myself before I walked into a horse's stall, for a single negative thought was enough to manifest a ton of horseflesh pushing against me like an avalanche. When I centered myself and pulled my fields close in to my body, I found that I could even walk right through the horses' blind spots without them so much as lifting a hoof. Much later, after my clients returned, I would teach my students what the horses had taught me about how to hold a space for healing. It was one of my most valuable lessons.

Whatever epiphanies the animals brought me by day did nothing to make my nights easier. As I had done when I was a child, I did the best that I could to crowd my troubles and my pain out of my life with work. Every day I was up by 7:00 a.m. to feed the animals. From there, I changed into my three-piece suit and went straight to my $7,000 a month executive job in Fremont. By 3:00 p.m. I was back at the stable where I changed clothes, stuck a straw in my mouth, toted feed, and played Calaban to the old dowagers and society women whose horses I was happy to look after. The society women taught me about prejudice, something I had never felt in my life before. They treated me like nuclear waste, afraid to meet my eyes or touch me, projecting the worst aspects of themselves onto me because of the job I held. I knew this because I could read all of their thoughts. Knowing what they were thinking didn't make the experience any less painful.

Nights at the stables were when my troubles came home to roost. I would linger outside longer and longer before I went to bed, studying the stars from the steps of my motorhome, saying goodnight to the horses, doing all of these things like a child asking over and over for water because it is afraid of the monsters that only it knows await under the bed. My monsters waited inside my motorhome. They knew that I had to sleep sometime. And they knew that to sleep I had to let go and then they had me.

At those moments I felt utterly lost.

The monsters were my own creations, my failures and my fears. They gathered around my bed to tell me that I'd

65

never be loved again, that I was a failure as a businessman, father, and husband, and that I was a failure as a healer. It was the last of these that bothered me the most. I had unwittingly bargained away everything that I ever cared about so I could become a healer, and now I had no clients. I couldn't understand it. I had learned so much and would gladly offer it all to anyone who asked yet no one came. I was so certain that this was what I was meant to do, what I had incarnated for, what I had died in other lifetimes to bring forward into the present time. The fear that I might have been wrong gnawed at me like rats worrying the ropes and stays that were all that held me together. If I was wrong then all of my dreams and visions, all of the pain that I had caused myself and others, all of it was pointless. This thought haunted me like no other.

I started to have bouts of uncontrollable crying. Like seabirds flying before a squall they were the harbingers of my approaching emotional breakdown. Finally I came completely unraveled, falling to pieces in a motel during a business trip to Seattle.

I had taken a ruby amethyst crystal down to the motel's hot tub with me. When I finished my meditation and lowered the crystal from my forehead, all the makeshift dams within me suddenly gave way at once. A huge wave of sorrow washed over me, followed by another and then another until I was shaking and crying like a baby. There was nothing that I could do to stop it. My tears were endless. I cried for all of the things that I had lost. I cried for my children. I cried for my parents. I cried for the love that I had squandered. I cried for the mere fact that I existed. The steaming water of the hot tub became my tears, the tears became me, and I became all of the sorrow that ever was until I was lost in an endless dark ocean of my own creation.

In the morning I awoke in a cold knot of clammy sheets in my room, unsure of where I was and with no idea of how I got there. I dressed shakily, went down to breakfast and read the menu over and over until the waitress asked me if there was something wrong. I blinked and shook my head, unable to speak. I felt so fragile that a single touch from her would have destroyed me.

My emotional meltdown in the hot tub created a space within me where I could look at my problems with perspective and clarity for the first time. After I got home, or more precisely to my motorhome, I spent some time thinking about what had gone wrong with my life and for the first time I could really see the role that polarities had played. I decided that I needed to somehow confront these forces that were making life so difficult for me. I would go out into the desert and I would take someone, the most evil person I knew, with me. We would call upon all of the polarities, positive and negative, and bring them to us so that each of us would be like the cathode and the anode of an immense cosmic battery, charged with the potential of all of the polarized energy in the universe. We would then shift all of the energies at once, sending them back to Source and bringing the universe back into balance, perhaps for the first time since its creation. I didn't know it at the time but my plan was seriously flawed; I didn't know it because I was still in polarity consciousness and could see no other alternative.

I had been to the desert once before, a year earlier. Angry and upset over what my life had become, I had marched out into the middle of Colorado's Great Sand Dunes National Monument, drawn a circle in the sand around me, and issued a challenge to the devil. I screamed every insult and provocation that I could think of but he never came. Instead, I heard a voice directing me to walk down a valley between two towering dunes. I felt sure that I was being asked to walk into the valley of the shadow of death, and I eagerly obliged, stalking along with my fists balled, ready to knock some sense into anything that got in my way. A huge dark snake, one of my biggest fears, lay motionless in the sand ahead of me. I stopped for a moment, and then stomped directly towards it. As I drew closer I saw that it wasn't a snake after all, but a gnarled piece of black wood that had somehow found its way into the heart of the treeless dunes. It was such a perfect facsimile of a snake that I had to kick it before I picked it up. I stuffed it into my backpack and took it home, where it remains as a reminder that the worst that the devil can do to me is activate my own fears.

I chose the desert again for my second trip for the same reason that they tested nuclear weapons there: There was no telling what might happen when we tried to deal with that much energy. For all I knew it could be a suicide mission. I'd seen the dark swirling colors of negative energy over Oakland before the fire, and over San Francisco before the quake and I knew what had happened when those energies changed form and became physically manifest. Whatever my misgivings, it didn't take me long to decide who I wanted to take with me. I knew of only one person who had more investments in the world of polarities than I did and that was the yogi I had known in California who purposefully invited negative energy into his Malibu ashram to accelerate his student's lessons. Although we hadn't parted on the best of terms—I had left his ashram at warp speed once I realized what he was up to, he appreciated my candor and the seriousness of what I was proposing, and readily agreed to come with me.

After I had thought about my multidimensional Manhattan Project for a little while, I started to have more and more second thoughts, just like the physicists connected with the original Manhattan project had done. When I conceived of the idea, I had assumed that as a beacon of righteousness I would be the positive side of the battery. The fact was that I had no guarantee that I might not be the opposite and this was extremely frightening to me. I started to feel as though I had volunteered to stand out in the middle of a golf course during a lightning storm while holding a five iron over my head. I was looking forward to creating a new era of balance in the world, not having my shoes blown off by negativity.

Somewhere in the midst of considering this problem, and not getting any answers in the way that I had come to expect them, I agreed to do a session with my old friend Lynn McFarlane. I'd known Lynn since I taught my first class at Drunvalo's mystery school in Questa, New Mexico. She came to me at my aunt's house, near the stables where I worked in Oakland. Although it was wonderful to see her again, I wouldn't know just how wonderful until the time came when she would present me with a gift that would completely change my life.

Almost as soon as Lynn and I had done the hypnotic induction together, and she had slipped into an altered state, I found myself head to head with some very powerful energy. I could feel it pressing down on me, like I was a thousand feet below the surface of the ocean. Using Lynn as a trance medium I made contact with the energy. "You better be ready," it sang out ominously.

The energy then went on to taunt me, as energies often did, probing me for fears and weaknesses that it could use to its advantage. It was immense and I was puny; it was powerful and I was weak; it was going to kill me and I was powerless to stop it. For some reason, rather than invoking my army of angels and wading into battle brandishing my sword of light as I had always done previously, I decided to try something new. I could always teach it a lesson. Before I did I wanted to really see it. I'd never really looked at these kinds of energies before.

With Lynn's permission, I closed my eyes and moved into the silence. Instantly I was in the center of a massive dark cloud that seemed to stretch for thousands of miles in all directions. Energy crackled through it like lightning. It wasn't kidding when it had said I was puny—I wasn't any bigger than a grain of sand in the Sahara compared to it. I had always thought that energies lied about such things. If it wasn't lying about its size, then perhaps it was serious when it said that I better be ready. I began to sincerely hope that I was.

I held my focus. It could kill me if it wanted to. I didn't care. I embraced my puniness—my life didn't matter anyway. What mattered was my essence. This was my proving ground. I had done battle with energies like this a thousand times, calling upon all of my legions of angels, the dolphins and the whales, and whoever or whatever else I needed to send them on their way. Now I realized for the first time why I felt that I had to work that way: it had to do with my fear about my own core energies, the belief that I couldn't be with these energies because I might not be balanced enough inside to resist them. For a long time now I had been preaching to my students about the importance of being love, and now I was on the witness stand and the question was being put to me. Either I was love or I wasn't: if I was love then there was nothing that this energy or any energy like it could ever do to me. I cross-examined myself. Mr. Page, I asked myself, are you love? Yes, I answered.

Instantaneously everything changed. The energy made a kind of a pfft sound, shrank to a tiny dot and disappeared like the image on an unplugged television. I looked all around me. I was alone in the great void. There was nothing positive or negative for as far as I could see. All that there was was in balance. I had let go of the polarities within myself.

From that day on, my life began to change. I canceled my plans to go out to the desert with the yogi. The trip was no longer necessary. I had learned that the entire universe is holographic. If we have pain inside then we see pain all around us, if we are polluted we see only pollution. I was no different. The polarities that I saw in the world around me were reflections, one and all, of the polarities within me. I had created a war outside of myself to mirror the war inside of myself, and now finally the war was over. I released St. George, St. Michael, Moses, and all of the guides and angels that I had recruited to help me with my work. They too were reflections, part of a stage play that I had written, directed, and cast myself. As above, so below. As inside, so outside.

I still had to deal with the mess that I had made of my life, but now that I was no longer a magnet for negativity it became much easier. There was light at the end of the tunnel. Mary, my wife, was one aspect of that light. We met when I helped to heal her horse at the stables. Soon after I met Mary, I met Shirley Holly at a workshop I gave in Texas. Shirley was the best student any teacher could hope for, and the three of us would found The Institute for Multidimensional Cellular Healing™. Within a year we were offered our own center in Houston, a mailing list of thousands of names, and I was in the flow of the universe again. It felt a lot better than trying to swim up Niagara Falls.

As balanced as I thought I had become, there still remained a piece of polarity lodged inside of me. Like shrapnel from a forgotten war, it would remain there for four more years, until I finally found the means to remove it.

Three years after I had released my polarities, I went back to Seattle to give a workshop. I had clients again, more than I had ever had before, and the people whose healing I facilitated came back to me again as students. I was also back at the site of my Waterloo. Shirley had, unbeknownst to me, checked me into the same room in the same hotel where I'd had my emotional breakdown, the nadir of my personal hell. I didn't know it but I had come here to learn about another kind of hell, the Hell that the fire and brimstone preachers talked about.

The problem with trying to frighten people into going to church, the way that the fire and brimstone preachers do, was that the fear had to be constant to keep them coming back each Sunday. The mechanism for this was to convince them that on some level they could never be entirely free of sin, no matter how hard they prayed, or how many times that they confessed. When these people died, their fear of being punished for their secret sins stayed with them. It made them turn away from the light, just as surely as if they had been in a satanic cult. Instead of going home to be with God and be whole again, many of them became hungry ghosts. Hungry ghosts desperately wanted to eat, smoke, be held, drink, make love or do anything that they could do in life instead of wandering around in the cold, loveless, darkness. When they found someone whose energetic fields were weakened, they moved in. If they had liked to drink, they would do everything they could to compel their hosts to drink, usually around ten times the normal amount because that's how much it took to make them feel the way that they had when they were alive. Other consequences for my living

72

clients (the spirits were also my clients) ranged from chronic fatigue to the re-creation of the illness or accident that killed the possessing spirit. Most of the people I saw had suffered with these consequences for years before they finally found their way to me. I think that if any of those fire and brimstone preachers had to experience the consequences of the judgments that they handed out so readily, from either the point of view of the possessor or of the possessed, they might never talk about Hell in the same way again.

Thus Hell was something that I didn't think about much, although I dealt with it all of the time. I didn't think about it because I didn't want to give energy to the distress that brought my clients, both living and dead, to me in the first place. However, during this particular workshop in Seattle, I would have occasion to think about Hell a great deal, and my thinking would lead me to do something which I have since become at least a little bit notorious for. I was a little bit notorious because I had only spoken of it once before. Perhaps writing about it will make me really notorious.

The opportunity to think about Hell came because one of my clients in Seattle had been there. I didn't know that we were going to Hell together until midway through her session when we began to look at releasing her patterns. After we looked at her death in a past life together, I asked where she went after she died. I always did this to make sure that I retrieved all of the pieces of my client wherever they were, and so that the client could understand the way that those lost fragments of themselves were affecting their lives today. I had seen spirits go to many different places after they died, from journeying to other planets to becoming a barnacle on the belly of a whale, but I had never seen one go straight to Hell, which is what she had done after she left her body. From what my client told me, it seemed that perhaps the fire and brimstone preachers knew what they were talking about after all. Everything was there: all of the despair, the torture, the hopelessness of the lost souls who believed in a God who would wish such a thing upon them. As I questioned her, eliciting more and more details, I soon saw Hell almost as vividly as if I had gone there myself. Visually, it was just as the medieval paintings depicted it to be—searing sulfurous smoke, forced labor, leathery-skinned demonic overseers, torture and misery wherever you looked.

I was already very familiar with the process of releasing trapped souls from prisons in other dimensions because of my work with witchcraft. It was relatively easy; the only real difficulty was finding them. I needed my clients to show me where the prisons were because these places didn't exist in space and time as we understood it. With my client in Hell, I could send the light to her, and we could hold a space for the souls to go home. It was very much like the way that the transporter beams worked on Star Trek.

I felt a familiar rush of energy as I held the gateway open. The cleansing light of Source flooded all of Hell, like a great ocean wave scours the shore, and then all was still. For a moment Hell was empty. There was great beauty in its emptiness. Like the shell of Alcatraz in San Francisco Bay, it had become, briefly, a monument to the freedom of those who once inhabited it.

My client's dark eyelashes fluttered like bathing birds in two overflowing saltwater pools: She had seen the beauty of it too. I leaned closer to her. "And how many years have you struggled trying to fulfill this mission?" I asked her.

"Centuries," she whispered. The trickle of tears cascading down her cheeks became a waterfall, ferrying away her fear and her pain, allowing her to be whole again. "Centuries," she whispered again. I held her forehead with my hand as we wept together. Hell was already filling up again but it was of no moment. I had the keys. She had given them to me.

Three nights later I padded down the hallway of the Rodeway Inn to the very same hot tub where I'd had my emotional breakdown. I twisted the hot tub's wall timer to the hash mark at sixty minutes. The warm water lapped at my chin like a chorus of puppy dog's tongues. I thought of all the tears that I had cried on that one lonely night so long ago. I had returned to the same room in the same hotel for a reason and now I knew what that reason was. Having triumphed over my personal hell, I had come here on a mission to change the collective version.

I'd had three days to ruminate about what I was going to do. Like some medieval cleric, I'd wondered first of all why God would permit such a place to endure for thousands of years. The answer had come to me right away, although it took substantially longer for me to fully accept it. God hadn't created Hell: Man had. Hell was just a thought form and had no reality beyond the energy of our beliefs, energy that had remained constant throughout history as long as stories were told about it.

The fact that Hell was only a thought form didn't detract from the massive constellation of suffering that revolved around it. It wasn't just the suffering of the souls who were sent there. There was immense suffering in the physical world as well that revolved around our belief in Hell. This suffering ranged from all of the people who lived their lives in subjugation because of their fear of it, to all of the physical facsimiles we had built of Hell—the dungeons, prisons, and concentration camps whose very existence was as much a function of our fear as the other Hell was.

It was the energy of our beliefs that made Hell real, nothing else. No other kind of hell could exist because if it did it would violate the sacred principle of free will. In essence, Hell was nothing more than a spell that we had cast on ourselves, and I was an expert at breaking spells. I had come to earth in the first place to release trapped souls and so that's what I did. I set all of the souls free that had cast themselves into Hell since the first release that I had done. Then I dismantled Hell, treating it just as I would a spell, creating a mirror image of it and then bringing the two thought forms together so that they canceled each other out in an instant. When I was done with Hell I moved on to Heaven. It was every bit as limiting a concept as Hell was, binding the souls of the dead to the imaginable whereas the true breadth of the universe was beyond imagination. Then I finished my soak, went to bed, and in the morning I woke up refreshed and had a nice breakfast.

A year later, I made the mistake of including this story in a lecture to a New Age group that had invited me to speak. I spent the rest of the evening responding to their attacks. People were upset and angry at what I had done. Evolved as they were, they still had investments in polarities and believed that some souls other than themselves deserved to go to Hell for their sins. I explained to them that their thoughts, and the thoughts of people like them, would have instantly recreated a new Heaven and Hell, and that Heaven and Hell would endure for as long as any one person on earth believed that they did. The only difference would be that the new Hell wouldn't be near as bleak, because we had evolved. Instead of throwing people into dungeons to be tortured to death, we probably housed them in huge motels with color TV's. "There'd probably even be a McDonalds down there now," I joked.

Nobody laughed. I might as well have been joking about evicting Santa Claus and paving the North Pole. Maybe they never planned on going there but at least they had always been able to navigate by it.

The fact of the matter was that I could no more destroy Hell than Satan could destroy me. All that I could do was change the collective consciousness of what Hell was, and probably only for an instant. This is how I believe human beings evolve. As a race we are the total of all of those tiny changes in our collective consciousness over the course of five billion years. Our shared reality is completely democratic, for this is the nature of oneness and this is what we have been struggling to bring into the physical world for centuries. Our votes are our thoughts, and in this sense we can choose to be conscious co-creators of our reality—creator-gods, or unconscious creators. Either way, we still create.

I had seen the world as a system of oppositions for more than forty years and I clung to those beliefs until they nearly destroyed me. Few of us, a man dying of AIDS had once whispered to me, learn anything by choice. I was no different. I had clung so stubbornly to polarity conscious-ness, first of all because my fear of death kept me there, and after that because of all of the energy that I was devoting to maintaining the polarities within myself. For as long as I saw myself as a self-sacrificing exorcist, as God's broom sweeping the world of evil, I had doomed myself to inhabiting a world where good and evil were in constant struggle, and my life became a conflict-riddled microcosm of this. The moment that I saw the truth of oneness, those conflicts in my life that I had created to validate my beliefs in polarities all but disappeared. Just as I was able to honorably discharge St. George and the rest of my angelic army, I was able to close a long chapter on my life and begin anew. The ensuing chapters would not be without struggle, conflict, and self-delusion, but it would be of a different type. I was one step closer to home.

∞ 6 ∞

The Planet

In 1993, I held my first-ever workshop in North Carolina. The workshop was a result of my fortuitously meeting Shirley Holly at one of my Uncle Drunvalo's Flower of Life workshops in Dallas. All of the clients who came to me for sessions at my workshop were followers of a certain self-styled guru whose channeled books have today made her a millionairess. The information in the books didn't come from any human entity, or even from a being in the angelic realms, but from extraterrestrials. She had a large following, some of whom moved to North Carolina to be near her. The hitch was that the beings that she channeled, who professed to love mankind, were also in the habit of abducting humans and experimenting with them. It was a major contradiction. My understanding of these beings is that they have completely lost their emotional body, and thus are incapable of compassion as we understand it. Love would thus be a completely foreign emotion to them. One result of this contradiction was that the guru's books and lectures were loaded with clever disinformation—some of it very dangerous, carefully wrapped in lesser truths. The other result was that some of the people around her really needed my help.

Of the forty five people I saw, every second or third person, was linked energetically to a race of lizard-like or saurian extraterrestrials. Groups of these beings were in my clients' fields, taking energy from them trying to control them, and basically making their lives very difficult. These beings claimed to live deep inside the earth and had about as much respect for us as the average human has for a housefly. They also claimed to have placed an energetic template on all humans to make us more like them, which would include our having tails. They regularly abducted humans to use in experiments, the main purpose of which was to create some type of hybrid being that they could then use to completely repopulate our planet.

After I heard these stories repeated more than a dozen times, I started to think that there was probably a way that we could help these beings find what they were looking for—basically the information that they needed to recreate the emotional body that they had lost or evolutionarily forgotten. I knew that the client that I was working with had at some point in time come from their reality to help them find this. Many people, I believe, have incarnated as humans to serve other races in this way.

I had the being that was speaking through my client take us to their spaceship so that we could give the vibration of the emotional body to its leaders directly, thus ending or completing whatever purpose they might have had on earth. The feeling of being on their spaceship was by this time familiar to me. I experienced it as a somewhat unpleasant heavy metallic feeling and an electromagnetic taste in my mouth. The beings' original planet had been destroyed but my client, as part of her mission, had during dreamtime found another completely uninhabited planet for them to live on while they completed the next state of their evolution. My client and I took every member of this race, and all of their spaceships, to this place together. When we arrived, we fulfilled our end of the bargain by giving them the vibration, the symbol, and the color of love. Then, I told them that I was placing a blue ring around their planet which would make it impossible for them to physically leave to find us again, and at the same time I was deactivating all of their space ships until such time as they had finished looking inward and had completed their evolution without interfering with other races. I stationed nine space ships from a space group that I was associated with around their planet, to make sure that the beings were not interfered with themselves.

With the lizard-like beings safely ensconced on their own planet, the rest of my sessions with the popular guru's followers were much easier. As is my practice, I didn't give the sessions any more thought or energy after I had finished with them. I returned home to California, and to my motorhome. Five days later, I was quietly watching television on a Saturday night when everything suddenly flew apart.

I felt a tremendous pain inside of me, as though one of my organs had somehow exploded and I fell down on the floor screaming. My wife Mary ran to kneel at my side. By this time I had curled myself into an agonized ball like a hurt caterpillar. "Hold my head! Hold my head!" I yelled. "I don't know what's happening. I don't know where I am."

At the moment I felt Mary's warm, caring, hands on my head, I found myself in another spaceship. Everything was in complete chaos. Alarms were screaming, the air was full of smoke, and I could see bodies, broken beams and electrical fires all around me. I found that I was looking at a man. He had an elongated head, large eyes, long thin fingers, and face that was shaped differently than mine. Nevertheless, at the moment that I saw him I knew that I was looking at myself as I existed in another dimension. This other reflection of myself looked imploringly at me. "Help us," it said. "You must help us." I stared dumbly at it. "Hold time," it pleaded urgently. "Just hold time."

I concentrated on doing as it asked. For a moment—and there was no way for me to know how long this moment was—everything was frozen. In that moment no more people died. Then, the next thing that I knew, one of the other ships had come alongside and was transferring the crew off of the doomed vessel that I was on.

The next image that I saw, was of myself in the rescue ship's sick bay. The otherworldly being that I had recognized as myself, was lying in a bed. While it was plain that he would recover, there was an immense sadness about him. Half of his crew, who were all like family to him, had perished in the explosion. I could feel what he was feeling and it was so powerful that I brought it forward with me into my own reality and the next thing that I knew I was sobbing my eyes out while Mary held me on the floor of my motorhome. I felt like I had just driven through a crosswalk and killed twenty students on their first day of school. It was awful.

It took me almost an hour to recover enough composure to talk. I only knew of one person who could hear what I thought had happened to me without judgment, and that was my Uncle Drunvalo. I called him and told him what had happened, that the planet that I had taken the reptilian beings to had suddenly become an inferno, and that when it exploded it had destroyed a number of the spaceships that I had asked to hold a space around it. Countless beings had died, not only the beings that I was associated with in that dimension, but also the entire race of beings that I had banished from earth.

Drunvalo listened carefully and sympathetically. I knew that the other worlds which I visited were as real to him as they were to me. He told me not to worry, that I'd do better next time. As trite as it sounded, there was really nothing else to say.

The following day, which fortunately was a Sunday, I was in mourning. I ate nothing, and stared out the window, locked into a kind of catatonia by the enormity of what I had somehow done. Then, just as the sun finds its way through seemingly impenetrable dark clouds after a terrible storm, I was given the understanding of what had really happened. From the way it came to me, holographically, I knew that it was something that the beings of the spaceships had understood perhaps only a moment before I did. The race of saurian extraterrestrials had chosen to explode their planet. They had decided to create their own ascension so that they could change form. Somehow, they moved their consciousness off of the planet and then they destroyed their physical selves.

The essence of the message was that what happened was not an accident. In fact, everything had turned out just as it was intended to. Knowing this lifted a great burden from my shoulders. From that day on, whenever I escorted a race of beings to another planet, I would place a white mist of forgetfulness around it. The mist would stop them from remembering me, my vibration, or anything connected with their experiences on earth. It would make sure that what had happened on that planet would never happen again. In the meantime, I could feel myself returning to life. I was hungry, and after I ate I would feed the horses.

∞ 7 ∞

Death

It had been raining in Oakland, where I grew up, and the sun had just come out to shine on my friend and me. The year was 1950 and I had just started grade one. We were playing in a shallow drainage ditch not far from my house. The dance of the sun's reflections and the delightful sensation of the cool pressure on the sides of my rubber boots, the earthy smell, and the constant murmur of running water were like a symphony to the two of us. By then, we both had specks of mud all over our faces that looked like extra freckles. We jumped in and out of the water, raced tiny splinters of wood, and reveled in watery innocent bliss until it was time to go home.

The next day, my friend's desk was empty. He had drowned sometime after I'd left him, playing in another much more dangerous flood channel on his way home. I was too upset to hear anything else my teacher said.

I was busy contemplating a horrible proposition, rolling it over and over in my mind, trying to find some way to disprove it. Somehow, I knew I had been responsible for my friend's death. I was the last one who saw him on earth and now he was gone and no amount of thinking that I could do on the subject could bring him back.

When I looked at his vacant desk, I'd never before felt so terrible and empty I resolved never to look at it again.

On each succeeding morning, my nanny would drop me off at school. I would wave to her and walk in the front door, just as I had always done. Then, I would do something that I had never done before. I walked straight past my classroom and out the back door. I was in mourning.

I found a kindred spirit in the kindly old man who ran the local grocery store. We both had a lot of time on our hands. Each day after I fled from my school, I helped him to clean the store and stock shelves. I found a treasure trove under the floor—a place where change magically collected, like it had been left for me by leprechauns. The truth was that the storekeeper had arthritis, dropped it, and didn't care to look for it. After work I'd draw my salary from under the floorboards and go to the Rexall drugstore next door to buy candy bars, my pockets jingling like sleigh bells. Sometimes I found as much as a dollar and a half, which would buy more candy bars in 1953 than I could ever hope to eat. Instead, I took them home and put them up in a dusty china cabinet at the end of the hall that my mother had forgotten about, where they slowly overflowed shelf by shelf until the cabinet had more sugar in it than the Hawaiian islands.

Two months later the jig was up. The school finally called my mother to ask her when I was returning. The drug store conveniently called about the same time to ask why I kept coming back. I showed my mom the chocolate bars. I was busted, but it didn't matter. I'd done what I needed to do to survive. I'd found solace in work and isolation. It was a pattern that I'd spend years trying to undo.

Much later, after my life had returned to normal, I allowed myself the pleasure of playing in the water again. Four years after that, another friend and I were catching pollywogs in a creek behind my house after school. The day after we played, the hospital called to tell my mother that my friend had contracted polio. I was rushed to the

85

hospital the same day to be tested. I never saw my friend again. He died only days after he was diagnosed. This was all of the evidence that I needed. I was a dangerous person to be with. This belief would complicate all of my relationships for nearly the next forty years.

My next major lesson about death came more than thirty years later, in 1984. The stress of running my multi-million dollar empire was causing me chest pains and a spreading numbness on my left side. My first fear was that I had some sort of heart problem, but after I had been thoroughly checked out medically, the conclusion was that my illness was in some way psychosomatic. My wife Rhonda recommended hypnotherapy. She had been seeing someone for help with weight control and was very satisfied with the results. Although I wasn't all that open minded back then, I decided I had nothing to lose by trying hypnosis. I couldn't have been more wrong.

The therapist's name was Fred Liedecker. He had an office in a beautiful old victorian house in the town of Middleton, where he greeted me warmly with a firm handshake and a welcoming smile. We sat down in his office together and I told him about the pain and numbness that I was experiencing. He asked me if I had any other problems. I took a moment to tote up my life. I was married to a beautiful woman who loved me, had two beautiful girls by her and two wonderful kids from my previous marriage, and I was worth several million dollars. I shook my head. Obviously, I had no problems.

Fred handed me a form on a clipboard to fill out. As I scanned the long list, I realized that I indeed did have problems. I had more problems than I knew what to do with. I'd just gotten so used to overwork that I'd come to associate all of the symptoms of the stress that went with it as normal.

Fred used a repetitive conditioning process to move me into an altered state. I stared at a candle, closed my eyes, opened my eyes again, going a little deeper each time. After about half an hour Fred had me right where he wanted me, laying in an altered state on his couch like a a a stalk of over-cooked asparagus. Fred leaned closer and said quietly: "Now look around and tell me what you see."

What I saw was a dark figure towering over me, at least eight feet tall, its face invisible beneath a drooping dark hood. From beneath that hood, unseen eyes impaled me like skewers. Blood roared in my ears like water coursing through a dam. I looked around desperately, but wherever I looked there he was. I was trapped, face to face with death itself. I knew that if it touched me I would die. I knew that if I didn't get away I would die. "Tell me what you see," Fred urged a second time.

I exploded off the couch. "I've had enough of this shit!" I yelled over my shoulder, as I pounded down the stairs like a linebacker. I heard Fred's voice plaintively calling after me as I nearly knocked his front door off of its hinges. Seconds later, my tires were screaming as I weaved down the road in a cloud of blue smoke, Fred's puppet-like figure bobbing and waving from the curb. I threw the jeep around a corner and drove like a bank robber for the interstate. I didn't slow down until I was safely home with the door locked behind me.

I had never looked inside myself in all of my life before and I didn't like what I saw. I stayed away from Fred, told no one what happened and worked harder than ever. It had always worked before.

Three weeks later I skulked back to Liedecker's office. I had tried everything I knew to avoid going back there but once the genie was out of the bottle there was no putting it back in.

Fred nodded sagely when I explained to him what had happened. What I had seen, he explained, was a communication from my subconscious. It couldn't hurt me but like an unopened letter from the war department, it deserved my full attention. I didn't completely believe him but the fact that I was still alive was evidence in his favor.

We went through the complicated induction a second time. "Now," Fred intoned significantly. "Look around and tell me what you see."

I gasped like a goldfish out of its bowl. It was still there. It had been waiting for me all along. I could feel those terrible eyes boring into me again like knives.

"Stay with it," Fred urged.

I could barely hear him. My body felt frozen. "There's no way out," I whispered. "I'm going to die."

"No, you're not," Fred insisted. "Ask this being what it wants with you."

There was no way that I was asking that being anything. All I wanted to do was get away from it, yet I knew that if I got up and ran away again it would only lie in wait for me. There had to be some other way.

Then it came to me. The only way out was through. Summoning all of my dwindling resolve, I stepped forward and past death.

All at once everything changed. I stood blinking in bright sunlight. I had a brief feeling of great peace and then a moment later I groaned out loud.

"Where are you now? What's happening?" Fred quizzed.

"Jesus," I murmured, "I'm with Jesus." Later Fred would show me the notes his wife had taken, which described the red stigmata that appeared on my wrists and ankles at that moment. I was on the cross with Jesus, in agonizing pain, gazing out with Him at the ragged crowd of people that had gathered to weep and gloat at His death.

Then I was a small boy lost in the crowd, watching in horror as the savior of mankind died with torturous slowness under a baking merciless sun.

The scene changed again. We were walking down a road together. He held one of my hands in His, and with the other I held a stick. I batted at rocks as we walked. Jesus looked down at me and squeezed my hand.

"You are my son," He said smiling. My eyes filled with tears and then suddenly I was back in Fred's office and the session was over.

I had posted death as my sentry, faithfully guarding the portal that led to my inner world. Until that day in Fred's office when I finally met his challenge, my world was completely external. I would move into these new worlds slowly at first, like a spelunker, not knowing what other tests I had designed for myself. Eventually, I would travel to worlds beyond my imagining, and when I did I would learn that there are many other ways of dying and that the road to enlightenment is paved with the bodies of our former selves. Whether I surrendered to this process or not would have no effect on the steady progress of the seasons of my life.

The stage was set for me to become a hypnotherapist. I had observed hundreds of Fred's sessions, completed a 200 hour certification course, and then enrolled in an advanced seminar with a gentleman named Bill Baldwin. At the time Bill Baldwin was one of the great pioneers of hypnotherapy, who along with people like Edith Fiore, was spearheading a movement that was taking hypnotherapists into territory formerly reserved for a few daring clergymen and the shaman healers of indigenous cultures. One of Bill's specialties was entity releasement, which was also the subject of Edith Fiore's landmark book, *The Unquiet Dead.*

Bill would begin by asking his hypnotized client a question like, "Is there anyone there with you?"

"Monty is with me," the client might reply. At this point a hush would generally fall over the class and we'd all lean forward in our seats—whatever your beliefs about entities were, they told some great stories. Once you've heard someone describe their own death, their adventures in the spirit world and their final reunion with God, well, you tended to stop reading a lot of fiction.

"Monty," Bill would ask, "What are you doing here?" Monty would generally respond through the client by saying something like, "I love her and I need to be with her."

Bill would glance down at his notes, or his assistant would help him to find the relevant passage. "Is this the Monty who died in 1965 in a car accident?"

"I'm not dead!" Monty would exclaim angrily. Bill would then regress Monty to the time of the car accident and have him take a look around. At this point the client might start to manifest some of the symptoms associated with Monty's violent death, in the same way that I had appropriated some of what Christ had been going through on the cross. Sometimes the spirits had done such a good job of convincing themselves that they were alive that Bill would have to hold a mirror up to the client and ask them whose body they saw.

"What's happening now, Monty?" Bill would inquire.

"I'm choking!" his client would gurgle. "I'm drowning in my own blood." This was often a very significant moment, as clients tended to recreate whatever illnesses the attaching spirit had died from. If this was the case, when the attaching spirit was released, whatever illnesses it had helped to create tended to clear up miraculously.

Once Monty had been convinced of the reality of his death, the fact that he was interfering with the life of whoever he had attached himself to, and that he couldn't evolve spiritually where he was, he might say something like "I'm ready to go now." Bill would then call upon his legions of angelic helpers, along with the spirits of the dolphins and the whales, to help transport the lost soul back to the light. The result, after all had been said and done, was very often a phenomenal healing on all levels. I couldn't believe that I was learning to do the same work myself.

Although I had heard Bill lecture on the topic and observed several sessions, somehow the truth of the entity releasement process had eluded me, until the one memorable day when everything suddenly became clear to me at once. The force of my insight brought me straight to my feet, like someone filled with the Holy Spirit at a prayer meeting. Bill stopped in the middle of a sentence to accommodate me. "Wait a minute!" I demanded. "Are you telling us that entities are spirits?"

Bill looked at me quizzically. He didn't normally take questions until the end of class. "Yes," he replied.

I fell back into my seat, thunderstruck. I don't know why I hadn't made that simple connection before then, but now that I had I felt like a blind man who had suddenly been shown how he could see. Entities were spirits who had somehow gotten lost after death. Spirits had souls. Spirit were therefore lost souls. I was going to be a rescuer of lost souls.

Not only did it all suddenly make sense; it was also magically exciting. The idea of rescuing lost souls and reuniting them with God resonated with me in a way that none of my various forays into business ever had. I knew right away that this was my true occupation, what I had come to earth to do, and I knew how to do it.

Feeling that I had more to learn about death, and something to offer the dying, I chose to volunteer my time at a hospice. Although I had told the people in charge that I was a hypnotherapist, I didn't tell them about some of the weirder things that I was into, such as speaking to the collective consciousnesses of diseases, or releasing entities. Hospices were very conservative organizations. In actuality they were businesses, and the last thing that they needed was a volunteer witch doctor running around upsetting their patients and donors. I didn't believe that I was a witch doctor, but there really wasn't any other way for people who didn't know me to understand what I did. We've forgotten the words for these things in our culture, like civilized Eskimos who have forgotten all of their words for snow.

My first client had cancer and was in so much pain that she was unable to rest. I was able to help her, and her evaluation of me to the hospice authorities bordered on the ecstatic. Soon, I had three clients assigned to me at once. I would see each of them in the evenings when I was finished with my jobs at the printing company and at the stables. It was a stressful routine, mainly because between my business setbacks and my separation from my wife and children, I felt I was dying inside at the time.

The end to my meteoric career as a hospice worker came when I was given the assignment of working with a nurse who also had cancer and like my first client was in constant unremitting pain. I followed the same winning strategy that I had used previously, which was to put the nurse deeply into an altered state and then ask to speak to the consciousness of the disease.

This time the cancer had an iron-fisted grip on her consciousness and had no intention of leaving. It refused to allow her to separate herself from it, and responded to any attempt that I made to budge it by creating waves of excruciating pain. The pain made communication between the client and myself impossible. I had to stop a few minutes into the session when it was clear that the energy would kill her before it would leave.

Naturally, my client's report to the hospice authorities was as damning as my first one was laudatory. The fact that my client was a nurse made her testimony even more compelling. No more clients were referred to me. I would continue with what I had learned but I would do it outside of the framework of any institution. It was time for me to learn just how much that I could do on my own.

I got my first assignment in 1991 as I relaxed in a hot tub at my mother's house in Fremont. My mom's place had become a kind of a halfway house for me after my divorce from my wife. I was lying back, mesmerized by the sound of the bubbles, and the dance of the earth and the stars, when suddenly it came to me. A voice spoke to me from deep inside myself and it said: Thirty million souls are about to be lost in Africa, and many more will die. These souls will be lost because of tragedy, fear and parents who refuse to let them go. Will you help us?

Yes, I answered immediately. I repeated it out loud to be sure. Thank you, said the voice politely. By the way, it added, you are from the Order of the Messiah. Then, whatever it was left, instantly, leaving me with pruned-up fingers and a head full of unanswered questions. How would I get to Africa? How could one man possibly help that many souls? My questions would go unanswered for almost nine months. In the meantime I searched for the true meaning of the word messiah. When I found out that it simply meant "messenger" I almost wished that I hadn't.

Dorothy

I didn't suspect anything out of the ordinary when someone who worked for me and knew of my unorthodox

93

sideline, asked if I could come out to Kaiser Hospital. Her mother was dying there. I met Dorothy, my employee's mother, in intensive care. Most of her immediate family had gathered there, as incarnated souls have always gathered, to see one of their number off or to greet a new arrival. In this case the vigil was not held by candlelight or in a temple, but under cool white fluorescent lights against a background hundreds of thousands of dollars worth of glowing and blinking electronic medical equipment, all of it completely impotent.

Dorothy's frail 80 year-old body had been lain to waste by a galloping cancer that had metastasized beyond the reach of any conventional cure. The medication that dripped constantly into her veins had rendered her virtually comatose. I could sense an awareness in her however, and a deep and overriding concern over the needs of her family. It was November and they were about to face their first Christmas without Dorothy there to unify them. Dorothy's worries about her family had kept her alive, and subjected her to excruciating pain in the process.

I set up ideomotor responses with her, touching her head lightly as I showed her the route that I wanted her nervous impulses to take to her feet. Communication was very difficult; it took several minutes to see a response arrive at her toes, and by then we were scratching our heads trying to decide which question it was that she might be answering.

In the years that had elapsed since I saw my last hospice patient, my technique for working with disease had evolved to a point where I could simply take the energy of the disease into my own body and release it back to Source myself. It was a strategy that had developed out of my work with children and animals. I soon found that it was often much simpler to work this way, sparing my

94

clients the trouble of understanding a different reality, and myself the trouble of dealing with recalcitrant energies on a level that might cause unnecessary pain. This is what I did with Dorothy. The family thanked me profusely, all of them noticing that Dorothy seemed to be much more at peace in her stainless steel bier.

That evening, when I went up to my aunt's house to clean up after my chores around the stable, there was a message waiting for me from Dorothy's family. She had been calling out for me. I turned around and drove straight back to the hospital.

This time, there was standing room only at Dorothy's bedside. Her family somehow knew that she would be leaving very soon. They were all there, just as they'd gathered at her behest so many other times in their lives. I could see all their stories written in Dorothy's old, lined face. They stood watching her carefully, like Moses' mother might have stood watching his little boat of reeds before the current caught it and took it away down the Nile. I cleared a small space at her bedside and sat down to do what I had been called for.

After I asked if anyone had anything to say to Dorothy before she passed, I leaned close to Dorothy's ear and led her through a meditation. In the meditation, she became an eagle, soaring on powerful wings in a clear blue sky, rising higher and higher. The higher she soared, the quieter the room became. I told Dorothy to feel the warm light of the sun in the air and on her wings, to breathe it in and feel it touching her inside, to feel the sun in every one of her cells. It was time. "Dorothy," I whispered, "you don't need air anymore. All is light. You have become light. Breathe in the light."

Like a newborn baby blinking in the artificial light of a hospital, I felt Dorothy breathe in the clear light of God for the first time. The heart monitor overhead began frantically bleating like a lost sheep. I heard gasps. No one in the room had ever seen someone given permission to die before. I stared at Dorothy. Something else was happening, something that I had never experienced in all of my life before either.

At the moment Dorothy took her light breath, the entire room began to vibrate with an energy more powerful than any I had ever known. There was a loud roaring, rushing sound as well. It felt like God was reaching right through me to gather up Dorothy in a great vortex of light and take her home. Then the entire room seemed to explode and suddenly I could feel the energy expanding outward, reaching all over the earth, until it had touched the entire planet. Then, just as suddenly, the energy drew inward upon itself and completely disappeared.

I blinked and looked around the room. The heart monitor still beeped incessantly, insisting that we all look at the flat line that was Dorothy's last signature. A nurse stepped forward and turned it off. All of the expensive equipment stood by without purpose, like disarmed sentries in an empty prison. A soul was missing. There had been an escape.

No one said anything. No one needed to. We had all felt it. I took a deep breath and excused myself, leaving the family to marvel at the empty vessel that lay as lightly as dew on the starched white sheets. Dorothy was gone, long live Dorothy.

I carefully closed the door behind me and made my way to the nearest chair. The vibration in the corridor had completely changed. It was as if the whole hospital and everything and everyone in it had been instantaneously bleached and steam-cleaned by the clear light of Source.

The people passing me in the corridor all had the same stunned beatific look on their faces as the people who had been in the room with me, as I no doubt did. We had all been touched together.

Somehow, in holding a space for Dorothy to die in, we had created an opening for the angels to come in. One third of the thirty million souls in Africa had been carried home in that incredible vortex. The time I had spent in reflection and meditation amongst the horses at the stable was to prepare me for just this moment. If I hadn't cleared myself so that I could become the "good hollow bone" that the First People spoke about, I would have been burnt out like a bad fuse by the force of the energy running through me.

I went back to the stables and my motorhome. That night, for the first time in a long time, I didn't think once about what I had lost, and how it felt to be an ex-millionaire, ex-husband, and ex-father living on a thousand dollars a month. It didn't matter that my life was a shambles. I was right where I needed to be.

Cindy

I thought often over the next few weeks of the 20 million souls who remained lost and how I could possibly help all of them. All I could do was wait for further instructions, or for another miracle, but when neither materialized all that was left for me to do was to go about my business. I continued with my daily routine, going to work in the printing company in the morning, and coming home to the stables to shovel manure, clean water troughs and tote feed bags in the afternoons. The contrast between my two stations in life was starkly reinforced by some of the wealthy patrons of the stable, who tended to treat me like I was something less than human. The horses, on the other hand, reacted to me with complete honesty and would tolerate nothing less in return.

Of all of the horses that I had charge of, Cindy was my very favorite. She was a big chestnut mare, slightly sway-backed at thirty-three years old, and wise beyond measure. She had wonderful eyes that always brimmed with compassion, like dark brown windows that looked out over heaven.

I knew something was wrong when I came back to the stables after work and Cindy didn't appear, as she always had done, to greet me. I found her lying on her side in her stall, unable to get up. Every attempt she made weakened her more and more. Even breathing had become an effort for her. She wanted to live more than anything. Her love of life burned fiercely like a fire within her. Even as she lay panting and exhausted, her heaving flanks flecked with straw and manure, that bright flame stubbornly refused to go out.

I got three people to help me turn her over. I could sense the numbness spreading through Cindy's side and down her legs. Every so often she would roll her eyes and try once more to throw her bulk over her center, heaving and kicking at the sides of the stall only to buckle and crash back down again. I watched her herculean struggle for two hours. She tried over and over and over again. Still she lay there like a great schooner undone by the tides. Both of our hearts were breaking.

I knelt down in the straw beside Cindy and gently stroked her head while I prayed. I called upon the assistance of all of my friends, the Native American spirits who had come to my home to tell me about Blue Lake. I told Cindy that they were coming to help, that they had nothing but love for her, and that they would do whatever she asked of them. Gradually, she relaxed and stopped struggling. Her breathing became quick and shallow; her lips began to pull away from her gums in a kind of grimace. I had seen this pattern in horses many times. It meant only one thing. It meant that they were about to die.

I heard a horrified gasp from behind me and looked up. Cathy, Cindy's owner, stared at the two of us, her hand held to her mouth. She knew what Cindy's grimace meant as well. "I'm sorry," I said lamely.

Cathy asked me to leave so that she could be alone with her horse for a few minutes. I passed the veterinarian coming in as I walked away from Cindy's stall. I nodded at him and he shot me a tight unhappy smile in return. He knew what he was going to be asked to do. I sat down on a trailer hitch outside of the barn, preparing to hold a space for Cindy's passing. A minute or two later I saw the vet striding stiffly out of the barn. He was going to his pickup truck to prepare an injection. There was nothing else left to do.

The vet walked back toward the barn, swinging his black bag with the big syringe full of poison packed safely inside. Cindy's earthwalk would be over in less than five minutes. At that moment I heard them. The sound of native american chanting was drifting out from the training arena. They had come, just as I had asked. They were dancing and singing in the arena, twenty or thirty of them, beautifully arrayed in buckskin, beads, bone, and turquoise. They had come to offer Cindy a reprieve. Then the vet walked right through them, on his way to execute her.

I wished that I had tagged along, just to see the expression on his face, because a few moments later Cindy wobbled out of her stall behind her proud owner. The vet trailed them doubtfully, still carrying the poison that he'd never had the chance to use. The dancing spirits had vanished. Cindy was no longer the horse any of us had known. She had become a miracle.

I had never seen any of my human clients cling to life with such tenacity, such love. So many of us, myself included, lost sight of why we had originally chosen to come here and longed to go back. Cindy, at the moment when she was about to die, had taught me what it meant to really be alive.

That afternoon Cathy called Terry Ryan, a noted psychic, to come over and work with Cindy. Terry's specialty was telepathic communication with animals. Cindy told Terry about the Native Americans. She said that they came to her stall and spoke to her. They said that all that she had to do was think about what she wanted to do and they would help to make it real. More than anything in the world Cindy wanted to get up. She tried again, as the native american spirits stood over her. The next thing that she knew she was on her feet, with her owner draped around her neck kissing her and weeping for joy.

Cathy shrugged her shoulders when she told me this story, as if to say maybe it was real, maybe it wasn't. She didn't care as long as she had Cindy. I cared a great deal because I knew it was real. It was so damn real that I wanted to run outside and scream it to the world until I couldn't scream any more. I didn't share this with her—I had learned to be careful about who I told about my reality. Instead, I nodded sagely and scurried off to be alone with my wonder and my excitement. My last doubts had been erased. I knew that what I had seen was real, that my guides and helpers actually existed, and that I was able to help bring them forward into the physical world. I knew that I had been part of a miracle.

Cindy did well for the next few months, ambling out to greet me, following me around the stable, and sharing her great heart with us as she had always done. Gradually, day by day, she grew weaker again. It got harder and harder for her to get up until once again the time came when she couldn't get up at all.

We rigged up a kind of tent to keep the sun off of her. It had rained the day before and the only ground that was dry was beneath the rubber mat that Cindy lay on. I labored clownishly in the sucking mud, sliding more mats underneath her whenever she tried to move.

Cathy and I looked at each other sadly. This time both of us believed it was hopeless. While she went to call the vet, I knelt down in the mud beside Cindy and spoke gently to her. I read her a poem that she had inspired me to write. The poem was about the importance of being alive. I told her some of the things that she had taught me and how I had learned to look at my life in a completely different way in the time since she had shown me its true value. I thanked her for staying to teach me these things.

I heard the steady squish squish of two sets of boots coming back to the paddock. The vet's shadow fell over us. He wore the same tight smile that he had worn the last time he had come for Cindy. The only thing that he liked less than putting animals to sleep was watching them suffer.

The veterinarian gave Cindy the injection. She took one last desperate gasp of air, the kind of breath someone takes after they've just been saved from drowning, and then I felt the same unexpected but unmistakable shuddering power that I had felt in the hospital with Dorothy. I felt it reaching through me to Cindy and then it exploded straight up and ripped outward to encompass the entire planet. Then, just as suddenly, the vortex pulled in on itself, like a tornado being pulled into a cloud, and all was still. Very still. Cindy was gone but instead of feeling empty and sad I felt full and complete. Satisfied.

101

I glanced over at Cathy and the veterinarian, trying to appear as though nothing out of the ordinary had happened so that I could gauge my experience against their reactions. I needn't have bothered to be surreptitious about it. They both looked like they'd just been struck by lightning. Cathy was the first to recover. She blinked the tears from her eyes and swallowed. "Kenny?" she asked. "Is she-" I nodded confidently. Cindy was most definitely gone. So was every entity for miles around. The trees looked like they'd just been washed, the mud and the manure that I was kneeling in felt sanctified, and every one of us was blessed. God's footprints were all around us. My mission was two thirds completed.

Grandfather

My grandfather had been diagnosed with cancer at about the same time that I'd first been offered the mission to rescue all of the lost souls. The cancer was spreading rapidly because he had refused to submit to chemotherapy. His wife of sixty years, my grandmother, had died two years earlier and my grandfather wanted more than anything to join her. He was a devout Catholic and in the last month of his life he confessed to me that at night when he slept the angels came for him to show him all of the wonders of heaven. As a consequence, he liked to stay in bed and dream rather then get up in the morning, something which caused the family a great deal of unnecessary concern. Finally, they called me to tell me that he had taken twice his normal dose of morphine and that they couldn't wake him up.

When I got there, I could tell right away from the sound in his chest that his heart was failing, and that he had little time. The priest that we had called paced around the bed nervously. "You're letting this man die," he complained.

"Yes," I told him. "We are." I made it clear to the nervous cleric that if he was uncomfortable he should leave and he quickly acquiesced. He was as scared of death as I had once been. It was fine: We didn't need him.

I climbed up beside my grandfather, like I had when I was a little boy, and held his head in my hands. "Grandfather," I told him. "All of your affairs are in order. There is nothing to keep you here now. You can let go with our blessings." I went on to lead him through the same meditation that I had taken Dorothy through. When I felt it was time, I told him to stop breathing air, and to take the light breath. He did exactly as I said. The gurgling in his pleural cavity suddenly stopped. Before I could take a breath, the energy descended upon all of us like a tornado. It was even more powerful than it had been the two previous times. The roar was almost deafening. Then the energy exploded outwards and I knew in my heart that the rest of the souls had been collected.

Each time the energy had come, the feeling had been a little more intense, had lasted a little bit longer, and the afterglow had been more pronounced. Whatever I was doing, I thought, I was getting better at it. My aunt would later say that my grandfather's passing was the most beautiful thing that she'd ever seen.

I had completed a circle, or more precisely a spiral of awareness. Only a few years earlier I had run screaming out of a hypnotherapist's office because I had seen the grim reaper and I was afraid. Three weeks later I had gone back to face my fear. I learned first from speaking to entities, and later seeing them, that death had no dominion beyond the physical body, that life was eternal. I moved on from helping individuals to die, to helping tens of thousands of souls to find their way back to the light. I had become a gatekeeper. I held a gate open by momentarily affecting time, creating a space in which miracles could occur. This would be confirmed for me when I found a tiny gate lying on the ground between my feet during my workshop near Montauk on Long Island in 1994. Now instead of running from death, I was in partnership with it and through embracing death I had come to embrace life as I never had before.

∞ **8** ∞

Flexible Flyer

Seven a.m., Pacific time. I was driving down the Silverado Trail from Livermore to my resorts at Clear Lake, where I had relocated with my family after the flood and the bankruptcy. Although I had driven this road many times before, the honeymoon between us wasn't over and I was still in love with the natural beauty of the area. I relaxed and enjoyed the view as the road wound its way through California wine country. I did a lot of my best thinking on the road, or in airplanes. I was a workaholic in those days, always finding new tasks to add to an already very demanding work schedule. With all of the things that I had going on in my life, driving had become a kind of meditation for me.

Something, an inner voice, asked me to pull over. I ignored it for a few moments while my conscious mind rolled through the usual rolodex of objections, not the least of which was the ten o'clock appointment I had to keep with one of my business partners. Running businesses under the protection of a Chapter 11 filing required keeping a lot of appointments, and running the businesses on a shoestring meant that I had to attend to most things myself, from payroll to carpentry. The voice immediately came back, stronger this time, demanding my attention, literally screaming at me to pull over.

I swung the wheel over and pulled onto a paved roadside cutout. I remember thinking that something wasn't right. My hand felt like it was made out of lead as I reached for the ignition key. I saw the steering wheel rushing up to meet my face. Then I saw nothing at all.

The first thing I noticed was that I didn't feel heavy anymore. I felt myself becoming lighter and lighter, until I could feel myself traveling through space at incredible speed, so fast that I couldn't even tell whether I had a body or not. I had a sense that I was bridging space in some way, leaving a trail like a comet as I rocketed from one point to another. Having no frame of reference to compare my experience to, not knowing whether I was awake, dead of a heart attack, or asleep, I didn't have time to question my experience, only to be it.

The sensations of depth, sound, and smell returned. I could now see thick clouds of greasy black smoke boiling up from the ground below me. Through the smoke I could see a hotel. I could see a grassy area across from the hotel, a swimming pool behind it, and an airport in the distance. There were no fire trucks or ambulances. Then the entire scene faded to black.

I was in a hotel corridor, full of roiling black smoke. The wallpaper was bubbling and peeling off of the walls from the heat. I could perceive something through the thick smoke, on the floor about fifty feet in front of me. I moved closer. It was a man, curled up in a tiny ball on the floor trying desperately to breathe. There was a silhouette beside him pulling frantically on his arm. I could sense that the silhouette, like the man, was very afraid. Although it was human in form, it was vaguely incorporeal, like something that you could put your hand through, and because of this it was ineffectual; the man wasn't budging. My inner voice told me instantly that this was no time to ask questions, that we had to get that man out of there. I knew it was not his time to die.

I felt my vibration changing and as I became more solid I could perceive just how desperate a situation we were in. The man, about 220 pounds, shirtless and gasping for air like a fish out of water, looked about as easy to move as a bank safe. I could see that the being tugging on the other shoulder wasn't going to be much help. In fact, I could see right through it.

Both the being and I gathered all of our energy and intent. We lowered our heads and hit that man like two football players at our first day of training camp, putting everything that we had into it. It wasn't just his life that was at stake. I knew that if we didn't succeed that I would die trying.

I looked about in shock. We had done more than just move. We were fifty feet further down the long hotel corridor, fifty feet closer to the fire exit. Looking back now, I know that I couldn't have been physically present or dense enough to move him through any kind of muscular effort. I could only have moved him psychically.

Encouraged, I looked over at the being that I had come to help. She was a young woman, slender, around 19 years old with blonde hair. Together, we lowered our heads, focused every ounce of our energy, and rammed the man again. I don't know how we did it, but the next thing I knew we were in the fire escape rolling, pushing and dragging the man downstairs.

Outside, the fire trucks and emergency vehicles had arrived. Two firemen ran toward the man we had helped, now coughing and retching outside the fire exit. The hotel was now a raging inferno. I stood in a grassy area in the midst of a ring of angelic beings. With me, within the semicircle, were all of the people that had died in the catastrophe, and I was talking to them. We had corralled the fire victims so that they wouldn't get lost. Most of them were confused, bewildered, and scared. Not all of them even understood that they were dead. All that they knew was that they had just been taking a shower, or sitting in bed reaching for the phone to call room service when suddenly everything changed.

I told the people that had died, that they were going to be all right, that their guides and angels were there and that we were going to take care of them. I had to make them understand that they were safe, that nothing bad was going to happen to them. They needed to know this so that they didn't run screaming out into the streets, which is probably what I would have done. If they ran away they would become lost, which was at least as bad as dying in a fire.

I started to talk to the angelic beings who were holding the circle around us. They were part of a hand-picked disaster response team. The hotel fire still raged behind me and more and more fire trucks and ambulances kept arriving. One of the firemen pulling a hose ran right through us. We didn't pay any attention to him. I continued my debriefing, carefully explaining to the angelic beings how they could be of better service to other victims by preparing for their missions more carefully, so that they themselves wouldn't fall victim to the confusion and chaos. They listened to me very carefully and when my talk was over, thanked me many times for helping them.

Somehow the fact that I was still present in the phys-ical made it possible for me to exist in a state between their world and mine, a state or a vibration from which I could do work that they couldn't do. I also knew that these beings would stay at the hotel as long as they needed to, until their work was done.

A produce truck whooshed past on the highway, rocking my car slightly in its wake. I pulled my head off the car's steering wheel, blinking owlishly at the faintly glowing digital clock on the dashboard. I had been parked for forty five minutes. I studied the green meadow outside skeptically. Something didn't smell right. My car in particular. It smelled like it had been on fire. I tugged my lapel under my nose and sniffed at it. My nose wrinkled and I recoiled slightly. My clothes smelled as if I had been sitting in a bar all night. They were saturated with smoke.

That night as I collapsed into my easy chair back at home in Livermore, the last thing I had on my mind was the forty-five minutes that I had somehow lost that morning. What I had on my mind was an hour of delightfully purposeless television. I let my mind float away as I channel-surfed. The sound of the blow-dried saccharin television news anchors was as restful to me as the babbling of a brook.

Then I snapped upright in the chair, as awake as if someone had dumped a bucket of ice water on my head. The lead item on the news was the crash of an air force jet on a training mission. I felt the goosebumps rising all over my body as I watched the footage shot from a circling helicopter of the burning hotel. The back of my neck felt like it had 1,000 volts running through it. There was absolutely no doubt in my mind. I had been there. I hadn't dreamed it. It was real.

From that moment forward, I never looked at dreams the same way again. The different worlds that I traveled between were starting to overlap. While my physical reality was breaking down, my invisible realities were becoming real. The smoke that I smelled on my clothes was as tangible as my money and my resorts. Previously I had experienced different realities only as fragments. Now I understood that each part contained the whole. As my reality was becoming holographic, so was I.

∞ 9 ∞

Bedeviled

Scam artists have always been my greatest teachers. The yogi was one of these. He came to one of the classes that I was teaching at my Uncle Drunvalo's mystery school in Questa, New Mexico. The yogi was a wealthy man, and presided over a large group of followers in Los Angeles. He had heard of me and my work, and was eager to learn all that he could about it. In his session, he kept asking the same question over and over. "There must be something between darkness and white light," he kept insisting. "There has to be. Aaah-chooo!" The yogi had allergies and blew his way through an entire box of Kleenex during his session. Finally it came to him.

"Clear light!" he announced triumphantly. "Clear light!" I knew that he was right. The concept of using the cleansing power of clear light, rather than white light which invites its polarity, has since become key to my work. I was in a small way indebted to the slight, sneezing man on my table; feeling that we had something to learn from each other, I would later accept his offer to come and teach at his ashram in Malibu, California. It was a decision that I would have reason to regret.

I was seeing clients at a hotel in Los Angeles on the day when the yogi invited me to come and work at his center. Of the six people that I had scheduled that day, the first three clients that I saw were all beautiful women. Curiously, they were all dressed to kill as well, like they had just stepped off of a movie set. I dutifully covered each of them with white sheets while I worked. At that point in my career, with my heavy investment in polarities, an instant's distraction could cost me dearly. Without my continuous concentration and focused intent, the hotel might suddenly find itself awash in uninvited guests, and far worse things were possible.

The phone rang minutes after I had finished with the last of the women. It was the yogi. Thirty minutes later, I was relaxing like a maharajah in the back of a white stretch limousine watching Malibu glide by through the tinted windows. If I had had my eyes open I would have seen in the improbably dressed women and the limo, warnings to me that all was not as it seemed. Instead, I thought that I had arrived. I would maintain that belief by draping a clean white sheet over everything I saw at the yogi's center, just as I had when I saw the women, until the time when the sheet was finally ripped aside.

The yogi's retreat was everything that he had promised, a secluded and tranquil paradise. The main house, where the yogi lived, offered a breathtaking view of the Pacific Ocean. Below the house were big permanent sleeping tents, gardens, a temple, and numerous outbuildings. The yogi had the rest of my day's clients delivered by limousine. I gratefully accepted his offer to spend the night. The next day I worked on his paramour, the most beautiful of all of the beautiful women who inexplicably filled the tents and the gardens on weekends. The yogi sat directly across from me as I worked on her, watching my every move. Halfway through the session, he leaned over her so that his face was inches away from mine. "How dare you," he hissed. "How dare you know all of these things that I've struggled for twenty years to learn." Intent as I was on holding a space for my client's healing, I assumed that the yogi was being ironic or clever. This was my second mistake.

After my session with Yonanda, his girlfriend, the yogi extended an invitation for me to stay with him permanently and teach. He had a beautiful cottage that I could live in and I could continue to see my paying clients whenever I wanted to. The teaching excited me the most. I wanted to teach more than anything.

My first student, not coincidentally, was Yonanda. She quickly became my constant companion, attending all of my sessions. As flattering as it was to be shadowed everywhere on the compound by such a striking consort, I didn't have time to think of the ramifications. Stranger things were happening.

The first thing that I noticed was that my possessions were somehow being moved. I had arrayed all of my sacred talismans out on the back porch railing of the secluded cottage the yogi had rented to me. One day, I looked out at my talismans, and realized that three of them—two wood carvings of a dolphin and a whale, and an antler carved into a fetish—were missing. All of the crystals and other items that I'd placed on the railing on either side of them were untouched. The railing itself overlooked the steep side of an arroyo, so that the deck was about fourteen feet off of the ground. There was no way that I could think of for either man or beast to get up there.

The dolphin and the whale were particularly important to me because they were the things that I would physically hold when my work made me doubt my sanity. I searched high and low, hauling myself up and down the slope of the arroyo by grabbing onto fistfuls of chaparral. Finally, I had to leave. It was Sunday afternoon and I had to drive for ten hours to get back to my weekday job at the printing company. I brought all of my remaining things in and put them on the coffee table. There wasn't very much that you could take from me at that point in my life that I would miss, except for those three little things. I couldn't believe that they were gone.

The next day a woman from the ashram called to say that my dolphin had been found. It was in a tree in the arroyo behind the cottage, at eye level with the balcony. Neither of us could figure out how it got there. Nevertheless, she retrieved it for me and put it with the rest of my things inside the cottage.

The wind was whispering of a storm over the mountains by the time I returned the next Friday. I woke up several times during the night to hear the cabin creaking restlessly over its wooden stilts like a ship dragging its anchors. One of the first things I did in the morning was to pick up the phone. I held the receiver close against my ear. Silence. I found the plug still in the jack, the wire severed with almost surgical precision. I pried the plug out of the wall jack with a screwdriver, got a new cord for the phone from one of the staff, and hooked everything up again, feeling a surge of relief when I heard the reassuring sound of a dial tone again. I made my phone call, got a busy signal, and decided to try later.

Ten minutes went by. I came out of the shower to find the line dead a second time. I yanked on the cord that I'd just installed. It'd been cut, again. My heart began to race. Someone or something had to have been in the room in the last ten minutes. It was then that I noticed that the dolphin was missing for the second time. What the hell! I thought. Why would someone cut my phone line and steal my dolphin?

Then I heard a low menacing growl. The cat that had moved into the cottage with me stared under the end table, its tail lashing back and forth like a bullwhip. I recoiled in disgust when I saw what the cat was staring at. There, in a kind of a cubby hole under the table was a big black rat, nearly as large as the cat. Between the rat's paws was my precious dolphin. The rat was methodically eating it.

I marched straight to the bedroom and my suitcase, where the small .22 caliber pistol that I'd carried since my run-ins with the bikers waited. I grabbed it and a flashlight. I was furious and I was loaded for rat. The rat didn't even blink at the flashlight, nor when I shot it, but the cat shot straight up in the air like a rocket. "Sorry kitty," I said sheepishly.

I lifted the top off of the end table and yanked my dolphin out of the rat's paws with righteous indignation. The cat pranced after me slavishly as I carried the rat out by its tail. I barely had enough time to get the rat safely interred and grab a glass of orange juice before I had to start my first class.

Forty students waited for me in the main house. Rats be damned, I thought to myself, teaching was my life's work. I asked what they wanted to work on that day. One of the four leaders, a woman—the whole place was run by women—spoke up and said, "we'd like to know what we were doing in our past lives." I felt like a magician at a children's birthday party. I rubbed my hands together to convey my workmanlike enthusiasm. They had asked me to do a trick that I knew how to do.

"Okay people," I announced. "Past lives it is." I cleared a space and arranged the four women in a circle, with their heads nearly touching and their feet facing outward in the four directions. "We'll all go there together." I led them all through a regression and had them envision themselves spiraling back through time. First, one of them started shaking, and then two of the others. I steadied three of the women and addressed the one whose life we were all going to explore.

"I'd like to speak to the dark energy around your head," I told the woman, "if it could speak to me now what would it say?" Instantly the woman's face contorted into a snarl.

"I'm angry at you!" she yelled. Right away I could hear shuffling all around us as the rest of the students discreetly moved back.

"Who are you?" I inquired calmly. My clients screamed at me all the time.

"You know who I am!"

"No I don't. Why don't you tell me?"

"You know who I am!" In between yelling at me she snarled, hissed and spat. I was used to that too. Her friends weren't. She was one of the most angelic-looking women that I'd ever seen, before I had anything to do with her. You could practically see her halo. Now she was rolling around on the floor and cursing like a sailor. I knew what most of them were thinking. I'd seen *The Exorcist*, too. That movie was nothing but trouble for someone in my business.

I switched my tack. "Where are you from?" I demanded. The woman spat at me again. I could hear an "aaah" from the crowd, like the sound you hear at the circus when the trapeze artist nearly falls off the high wire.

"Where are you from?!" I demanded again, raising my voice for emphasis. The woman smiled smugly at me.

"I was in the rat!" she snarled.

That was nearly enough to knock me off my high wire. I took a deep breath.

"Who are you?" I asked again. My client writhed and shook her head from side to side, presaging an utterance of great significance. You could practically see it traveling up her throat like a UPS truck.

"I am the DEVIL!" she yelled triumphantly. The crowd went "aaahh" again, expecting the worst, but now I had a foothold, something to work with.

The demonic energy had been around the compound for years, moving from person to person, leaving when they felt centered and entering their fields again when they were vulnerable. When it was between people, it attached itself to the rat, and when it saw an opening it would jump like a flea from the rat to another one of the yogi's acolytes.

"Being in negative service for thousands of years is hard work, isn't it?" I asked encouragingly.

"Yes," it admitted.

"Are you ready to go home now, to a place where you can be more than you ever could here?"

"Yes," it said simply. It was over. I looked around the room and asked if anyone had any questions. There were many. I had some too. For the yogi in particular.

I opened my eyes and ears around the ashram after that. One of the first things that I noticed was that there was an omnipresent sound to the place, emanating from high fidelity speakers secreted in the high corners of every room like spiders' eggs. The sound was a kind of a low-pitched choral hum. It was somehow very familiar; I knew that I had heard it before.

I strolled back to the main house for dinner that evening, lost in thought. A group of women from my class waved at me. I waved back absently. I'd never seen so many beautiful women in one place in my life. They were all over the grounds, laughing, talking, and doing exercises. I felt like a guest star on *Baywatch*. "Is something wrong?" a voice said from beside me. I felt a gentle touch on my elbow. Yonanda had slipped free from a group of women doing yoga to walk beside me.

I shook my head. "Just thinking," I told her.

"You know you're our golden boy out here," she said. "The yogi thinks so much of you. It's important to all of us that you're happy."

Gears were spinning inside my head like in an antique cash register during a white sale. Golden boy, golden boy, golden boy. I turned the words over and over in my mind. Finally I rang up a total.

"Excuse me," I told Yonanda. "I just thought of something that I need to do." I disengaged myself from my shadow and jogged quickly up to the house. I knew where I'd heard that sound. I'd heard it in a movie called *The Golden Child*. In the movie the noise had been described as the sound of pure evil.

I caught up with the yogi as he strolled like an old patriarch through the dining room, hands clasped behind his back, surveying the meal preparations. He smiled warmly at my approach. "Listen," I told him. "I just realized something." I went on to tell him all about the movie and the meaning of the chanting. I pointed up to where the sound seemed to be coming from in the dining room. "That's the same sound," I told him.

The yogi smiled and nodded. "Yes," he told me. "It is. I use that sound to attract evil."

"To attract evil?" I repeated incredulously. "Why on earth would you want to do that?"

"Why to accelerate my student's lessons of course," he told me, acting as though it should have been obvious to someone like me all along. He lowered his voice to a conspiratorial whisper. "Would you like to see my shrine?"

I dutifully followed him upstairs to his oversized master bedroom. It was like a temple in and of itself, beautifully furnished, with rows of votive candles burning 24 hours a day. He stopped in front of the doors to a big walk-in closet. I could feel the energy that emanated from inside. It was like walking into a wall. The yogi threw open the ceiling-high doors with a dramatic flourish. A row of shelves extended from the floor to the ceiling like bleachers. The shelves were completely populated by statues of Hindu deities. The statues were paired, so that beside each positive deity was its corresponding negative aspect. The energy washed over me like a wave. I took a step backwards. I thought about what students would have to go through in a place like this, with so much negativity all around them. And here, at the center of this energetic maelstrom, was the smiling cobra in front of me, bobbing and rubbing his hands together as he lectured excitedly about the rows of deities he had harnessed together to accomplish his ends.

I left that night, chagrined and a little wiser. Everything had suddenly become much clearer. I realized that my first student and constant shadow, the yogi's paramour, had really been sent to spy on me with the intent of eventually seducing me. The yogi saw my knowledge as power and wanted all of it. In my excitement over teaching, I hadn't noticed any of these things. I had ignored all of the subtle messages and it had taken a huge demonically possessed rat to convince me that all was not as I wanted it to seem.

Months later, I would find out that I had only begun to plumb the debts of my naivete. The beautiful women that descended on the ashram every weekend were prostitutes, each of them paying two thousand dollars a week to the guru for the pleasure of HIS company. He used the white stretch limousine that he had bought from a country music star to kidnap them, ostensibly for the purposes of rehabilitation. He fed them, took care of their health problems, weaned them from their addictions, and taught them basic spiritual truths. When the women "graduated" from the rehabilitation program they were no longer streetwalkers hectoring cars on Sunset Boulevard: they had been transformed into radiantly healthy experts in tantric yoga, and they were thousand dollar a night call girls. Most of them remained totally devoted to the yogi. They helped bring in new converts; those who weren't prostitutes were asked to give the yogi all their worldly possessions as proof of their dedication. Several of the women were executives in the yogi's network of companies, all of which he had a very safe arm's length relationship with. It was a smooth operation that had made the yogi a millionaire many times over. The woman who told me all of these things set out to destroy him, but only succeeded in dislodging him from his Malibu ashram. As for me, I was to have one last encounter with Lucifer in physical form.

In the Fall of 1994, I was giving a three-day workshop on an island in Puget Sound. My comrade in arms, Shirley Holly, and I had just finished a full day of sessions, only to find out that the well at the compound where we were working had gone dry. Psychics get "dirty" doing their work just like gravediggers do, and the idea of going to sleep without a bath or a shower was inconceivable, so we drove across the island to soak at a hot spring before turning in. I had to drive slowly on the way back because of the combination of no streetlights, no moon, and fog rolling in from the ocean.

Shirley tugged urgently at my sleeve. "Look at that!" she whispered excitedly. I had already seen them. Two hitchhikers stood improbably on the road that had been deserted when we drove to the hot springs forty-five minutes earlier. "Look at them, Ken," Shirley whispered again, still tugging at my sleeve.

"I see them, Shirley," I answered, as we both peered intently at the two figures.

"I'll just ask them if they're all right," she said, as though we had already agreed on a strategy. She rolled down her window halfway, like we had a dog in the car that might jump out.

"Of course they're not all right Shirley," I said. "We'll give them a ride."

Shirley's hand froze on the window crank. "Are you crazy?" she demanded. Shirley and I had worked together for years and she knew me better than just about anyone else except my wife, Mary. She had watched hundreds of my sessions before training as a practitioner herself. Having her ask me if I was crazy really meant something.

Shirley wasn't just concerned because I was about to pick up two hitchhikers on a deserted island road at midnight. The circumstances were ordinary compared to the hitchhikers themselves. The man introduced himself as Daryl, and winked broadly at me. He wore fingerless gloves and a satin cape over a tuxedo. His jet black hair was pulled back in a tight ponytail, his skin was as white as bone china, and he had eyes like two lumps of obsidian. His consort, who was ravishing, wore a mink coat, nylons, and high heels.

We'd hardly driven a mile down the road with them, when a strange unsettling feeling overcame me. I felt like a giant centipede was crawling up my back. Daryl was the name of the character that Jack Nicholson played in the movie, *The Witches of Eastwick*. Daryl was the devil. Daryl was in my car. I knew his vibration intimately from all the work I had done. Shirley and I glanced at each other. She had kept both of the passengers in the back seat engaged with a rapid fire series of inane questions, a sure sign that she was scared. The headlights washed over a rusted telephone sign. "We have to get out here," the man in the back said urgently. I slowed the car down.

"Here?" I said skeptically. Apart from a single light over the pay telephone, the building by the side of the road was obviously deserted.

"Stop," he demanded. "Stop." He bent over my window to shake my hand after he got out of the car. "God bless you," he said, letting the words drip with meaning. We watched them glide into the deserted building together and disappear.

Shirley cranked up her window with incredible speed as we drove away. She turned in her seat to stare at me accusingly.

"Do you know who those people were?" she demanded.

I nodded my head as I drove. "Yes," I answered evenly. "That was Lucifer."

"Well, I can't believe that you picked him up."

I had been thinking about that. What was he doing on that road and why did I pick him up? I had an answer. "So I could shake his hand," I said finally. We had come full circle, the devil and I. I no longer felt that I needed to call upon my legions of angels to hold him at bay. I no longer felt that he could kill me. We were no longer at war. Like a favorite teacher, he had come all the way to this small island to deliver me my graduation present. He had come to shake my hand.

∞ **10** ∞

Blue Lake

The haunting sound of the words "Blue Lake" chanted over and over that I had heard one night in my backyard at Clear Lake continued to echo in my mind long afterwards. A few months after I heard the chanting, in 1985, I felt compelled to write to the Taos Pueblo to ask permission to take my crystal to Blue Lake. I also felt compelled to enclose another crystal from my collection with the letter, as a kind of a token and as a way for them to experience my vibration. About six weeks later, I got a letter back from the Pueblo. The imposing letterhead read: War Council. The War Council, the letter said, had met to consider my request but for reasons that they were unable to share, they could not permit me to go to Blue Lake at this time. The crystal that I had sent them would be waiting at the pueblo offices anytime that I wanted to come and pick it up.

I was disappointed. It seemed immensely important to me to bring the crystal to Blue Lake; I had felt sure that the wise old men of the pueblo would see the truth of this as well. I was weary of presiding over my bankrupt businesses and wanted to accomplish something that would give my life meaning again. When I looked for a silver lining in the cloud that had descended around me, I thought of my Uncle Donny.

When I was four years old, my mother moved back to my grandparents' house in Oakland to regroup after her divorce. My grandfather was Donny's father. Donny was eight years old at the time, and I was a nuisance to him, but I followed him around like a puppy anyway. The essential nature of our relationship remained unchanged for many years. I would trail him around just as doggedly whenever our families co-mingled for the various holidays that held meaning for us. Finally, the war in Vietnam sundered us, as it sundered so many other families in the 1960's. Donny was called up early, in 1961, and I didn't know what happened to him afterwards other than that he stopped coming home to Oakland for Christmas. Our lives diverged from that point forward: unlike Donny, who was drafted, I enlisted in the National Guard and eighteen months later I was working my way up through the ranks of General Cable, on my way to becoming a millionaire.

Donny's unexpected life after the war, was the fulfill-ment of a pattern that began when he was born nearly seventeen years after his closest sibling. You never knew what Donny was going to do, was all my grandfather would say. Donny sent them postcards from places like Afghanistan and Tibet, and only my mother, a lifelong Rosicrucian, seemed to have any idea what he was up to. For my part, when I thought of him I remembered his legendary chariots: the new black 1958 Chevy my grandfa-ther bought him when he was 16 and the MG Midget he bought the year after. Washing Donny's MG when I was thirteen was one of my earliest religious experiences.

Now, our paths were coming together again. I had an exciting new job running a hologram company, and my vision of creating a hologram of Jesus required me to travel to Santa Fe to oversee the creation of the detailed miniature sculpture that I planned to photograph with laser beams. I knew that Donny was living in Taos, New Mexico, and I resolved to look him up. I knew next to nothing about crystals and something had told me that Donny was the man that I needed to talk to.

I pulled up outside of Donny's place in my rented Lincoln Towne Car, nattily attired in one of the many dark three piece suits that I wore like uniforms in those days. He lived in a small one bedroom house, at the end of a long gravel road, next to a weathered converted school bus that he used as a guest house and office. Several cords of wood were stacked up under the eaves advertising the coming winter.

The door swung open. A man stood in front of me who had shoulder-length hair and a beard like a hippie. The warm air drifting past him smelled of wood smoke and incense. Was this my uncle? I stuck out my hand. "Hi Donny," I said. "It's Ken."

Donny studied me solemnly as he returned my hand-shake. "I knew that someone from my family was coming," he replied, "I just didn't know who." He looked at me some more and then I followed him inside. "I need to tell you a story," he said. I sat down and got ready to listen. I liked stories.

Donny told me about the year he spent living off of the land in British Columbia in 1971. The story ended when he was poisoned and died. He held me in his steady gaze waiting to make sure that what he had told me had taken root. "Donny is dead," he explained seriously. "I am Akbar now." I understood. Akbar was the being that had come in to inhabit his body after Donny left. It was like a sublease. I understood subleases. My uncle didn't take his eyes off of me.

"Akbar," I said experimentally, trying out the feel of it on my tongue. No problem. Instead of my ultracool Uncle Donny I now had the wise and mysterious Uncle Akbar. Everybody should be so lucky.

Uncle Donny was Uncle Akbar for only a few years. Today he's widely known as Drunvalo Melchizedek. Until I met Drunvalo I had thought that a walk-in was someone who showed up for a haircut without an appointment. A walk-in, I learned, was the name popularized by the writer Ruth Montgomery for a soul who enters a fully grown body without being inconvenienced by the birth process. In essence we are all walk-ins; ours is a fairly young universe and we all came here from somewhere else. I have since come to believe that a walk-in is almost always a higher aspect of the original birth soul, after I went through the process myself. People, I would find out, changed all the time.

Once we got past the formalities, I found out that Drunvalo really did have a lot to tell me about crystals. The first thing that he told me was that they weren't just rocks: They were living beings, growing and changing all of the time. He showed me how to glean information from a crystal, by holding it to my forehead while mentally asking it a question. He also explained how crystals could hold immense amounts of energy, either positive or negative, and could thus be used either to hurt or heal people. They had even, he said, found out how to trap all of the energy of a nuclear explosion in a tiny crystal that you could hold in your hand. Now as in antiquity, crystals were still the ultimate weapon. The next day he introduced me to Katrina Raphael, who wrote the book *Crystal Enlightenment*, and two companion volumes. We spent the day hiking and she told me even more about crystals. By the end of the trip I couldn't think of any more questions to ask about them. On the evening before I left, Drunvalo made me a gift of a crystal he had been holding for a year and a half, and a book, *Joy's Way* by Brugh Joy. He touched the crystal. "I didn't know where it was supposed to go," he said, "but now I see that it belongs to you, Ken."

I had to come back up to northern New Mexico a few weeks later and this time Drunvalo came with me when I went to the offices of the Taos Pueblo to retrieve the crystal that I had sent with my letter. A big barrel-chested man with smiling dark eyes called out to us as we stepped out the building. Drunvalo introduced me to Jimmy, an old friend of his who lived on the pueblo. He and Drunvalo knew each other very well, although there were long spaces in their friendship occasioned by Jimmy's bouts with alcohol. At the moment, Jimmy was on the wagon and bone dry. He nodded seriously when I told him about my failed attempt to get permission from the pueblo to go to Blue Lake. "I was there, man," he said. "They said no because they're worried about witchcraft going on up there. That place is too powerful. Can't take chances."

In fact, as I later found out, they were careful enough to post armed guards over the trail most of the year. When I found out more about Blue Lake I was glad that they did. Not only was it a very powerful place, but it was linked energetically to other sacred sites all over the world. The Taos Tribe was right to protect it.

I took out the crystal that the war council had returned to me unopened and handed it to Jimmy. It was beautiful, clear, and double-terminated. I knew right away that I had to give it to him, and so I did. Jimmy held it up to the light and admired it. A smile stole over his craggy features like the sun coming up over a mountain. "I'll take you there," he suddenly announced. My heart jumped like a fish after a fly. Drunvalo slapped me on the back and hooted. We were going to Blue Lake after all.

A few weeks later, around the first of October, Jimmy called me in California. I rented a Towne Car again in

Albuquerque and drove up to Taos. Jimmy lived in an old double-wide trailer that the wind ripped through like cheesecloth. We sat up and talked as the wind whistled all around us and the propane furnace roared ineffectually at it like an old bully. Jimmy told me about Perona, an old man of seventy-six, the Kiva Indian, who was in charge of the spiritual education of the young children on the pueblo. Perona was so knowledgeable that he could spend an entire month just teaching the children about the sun and the moon. Although Perona was Jimmy's uncle, they were as close as father and son, and so it was natural for Jimmy to tell the older man about our planned trip to Blue Lake. Perona was instantly very concerned about what we were doing. The night after he talked to Jimmy, he placed two crossed eagle feathers across his chest and asked for a medicine dream to show him the truth of what we were attempting. The dream brought good news for all of us. Perona told Jimmy that what we were doing would change the world, and he insisted on coming. By that point, we were all very excited. Neither of us thought for a moment that the journey we were attempting might possibly be dangerous. The only sign I had that anything was amiss was the unseasonably cold weather and the fact that Jimmy told me they were having trouble catching the horses.

The next morning we drove up to Jimmy's "ranch" in his old pickup truck. His ranch was really just a lean-to and a corral on the land where he kept his animals. Perona was already waiting there for us with only two saddled horses. There were three of us. I looked over at Jimmy in shock. He shrugged. It was a famous shrug that many native people affected. The shrug contained the entire history of his people. It was a shrug that acknowledged the theft of everything they owned, the murders of

127

their grandparents, the pain of seeing the daily rape of the earth by men who cared nothing for it. It was a shrug that put one missing horse in its proper perspective.

Perona greeted me warmly, and made a few jokes about the weather. I could tell right away from looking at him why he knew so much about the sun and the moon: The three of them had obviously spent a lot of time together. His gray hair was pulled back in a braid, and had deep laugh lines around his mouth from a lifetime of smiling. It was plain that losing a horse meant even less to him than it did to Jimmy; they were both as tough as tempered steel and would have walked barefoot if they had to. Both of them were wearing just jeans, cowboy boots, and light plaid wool jackets, even though it had been raining since before dawn. I was completely charmed by their refusal to be ruffled by the most adverse of circumstances. It was shining evidence of their faith in the Creator. Being charmed didn't stop me from handing out the two rain ponchos that I'd stuffed in my pack at the last minute.

Jimmy's girlfriend pulled the truck away in a cloud of blue smoke. I watched the heated cab and the taillights recede down the snow-covered road and wondered what I'd got myself into. A few moments later we were off, with me hanging grimly onto the saddle behind Perona like somebody in a western who had lost his horse in a poker game.

Things didn't look too bad, at first. The rain gave way to huge wet flakes of snow that floated down slowly like cinders from a great fire somewhere beyond the clouds. The trail, which led to a picnic ground by the side of a river, was wide and well trodden, and a little ways down it a great snowy owl flew across the river in front of us, its majestic wings beating with hypnotic slowness. We exchanged knowing glances. We all knew that owls were powerful medicine animals.

What I didn't know was that the Lakota believe that the owl, which they call Hinhan, represents death, calling the name of those whose time it was to die. The owl spirit, Hinhan Nagi, guards the spirit road that leads to the milky way. Those travelers that weren't ready for the journey it hurled back down to earth to become wandering ghosts. Before the day was out, this story would acquire a kind of uncanny resonance for me.

Once we passed the snow-blanketed abandoned picnic site, the trail all but disappeared. I looked between Jimmy and Perona for clues but they continued to impassively urge the horses forward. We were following a river up to Blue Lake rather than taking the usual trail because of the weather. Plainly, no one else had taken the river route in quite some time. The trail was blocked over and over by blown-down pines that had obviously been there since the previous winter. We had to cross and recross the river over and over to get around them, and each time we did it got harder and harder to pick up the trail again in the snow. My down jacket was turning into an expensive feather sponge and Perona's jeans were dark down to his knees from the melting snow. The banks of the narrow defile we were in rose up gray and foreboding on either side of us like the walls of a prison as the horses clattered from one side of the shallow river to the other.

Finally, the trail seemed to completely disappear and we paused in the riverbed to confer like thwarted bloodhounds. The breath of the horses steamed faintly. I thought about the water that coursed around their ankles and how it was propelled upward by their energy and how it would fall again as rain and eventually find its way back to its mother the sea. My reverie abruptly ended as I felt the back legs of the horse buck hard underneath me. I peered upwards. The trail, it seemed, went straight up the embankment. I couldn't see Jimmy anywhere.

I stared apprehensively around Perona's poncho, my knuckles white around the edge of the saddle. A ragged line of gray circles in the snow broadcast Jimmy's progress, longer streaks telegraphing where his horse had slipped on the slick wet rock beneath the snow. He had already gained the ridge over the river and was lost in a bend among the trees but our horse was balking. Jimmy's horse had slipped and it had carried a balanced load of only half our weight.

Perona grunted and urged the horse forward with his legs. It trembled beneath us, drawing every muscle as taut as a bowstring in an effort to stop us all from sliding backwards as we jerked and lunged our way up the side of the embankment. I glanced nervously back at the dark outline of the river where it scissored through the snow thirty feet below. Perona spoke reassuringly to the horse, encouraging him forward again. Then all hell broke loose.

The horse lunged desperately as it started to slide backwards. Perona hollered at it. The horse kicked backwards and then my head slammed into Perona's back as the horse's hooves flailed desperately at some unseen beast in the air in front of us. The next thing I knew the ground was a white blur rushing up at me and then I was rolling down the side of the defile. I fetched up hard against a stump. Still in one piece and anesthetized by adrenaline, I jumped quickly up to see if Perona was okay. He wasn't.

I saw Perona twenty feet above me, bent low over the horse's neck as it trembled and shook beneath him. The slope beneath them was as steep and as slick as a wet slate roof. Perona clung to the horse's neck and whispered in its ear as it snorted and blew steam out of its nostrils. It jerked forward spasmodically like it was electrocuted and then started to slide backward in earnest, scrabbling helplessly against the black wet rocks beneath the snow until it slid backwards into the carcass of a big blown-down pine that we had crossed on the way up. They stayed there for a moment—the horse, the rider, and the tree—all balanced together like some improbable circus act.

The dead tree creaked and shifted like an unruly sleeper. The horse panicked and reared up. I saw it teeter on its great trembling back legs like a movie stallion, and then horse, rider, and tree all parted ways. Perona flew backwards through the air like he was shot from a cannon, landed hard in the rocks, snow and gravel ten feet below me, and somersaulted out of view. The horse, twisting in midair like a leaping dolphin, landed on its side with a sickening thud and rolled, flailing helplessly down the embankment to finish up thrashing and screaming in the river. I heard a low rumble and the sound of splintering wood above me, and turned just in time to see a dark greasy slick in the snow like it had just been plowed and to feel the impact as the dead pine tree slid into the backs of my legs and pitched me forward.

I saw myself throw my hands out just in time to stop me from opening my head up on the gray rock that jutted cruelly up in front of me like a shark's dorsal fin. I felt nothing. I had left my body to watch the whole thing from a safe perch far above the creek.

I knew right away that I'd died here before at this very spot, on that very rock, in a past life and I had fled my body before I had to relive it a second time. I saw myself struggling. My foot was pinned behind the stump, leaving me hanging face-down over the side of the gorge with my leg at an impossible angle. Perona was on his hands and knees in the river, shaking his head while water streamed off of him. The horse had just struggled to its feet and was staggering around in shock like a foal that couldn't find its mother.

I heard a muttered curse from Jimmy who had ridden back to see what all of the crashing and screaming was about and then I was right back in my body, suspended helplessly over that killer rock, trying to stem the pain in my leg by holding onto a dry branch over my head. Jimmy ran up to me and tried to shift the tree but it was hopeless. It was as long as a telephone pole and the roots were jammed down in the riverbed. Perona was on his knees in the water, holding onto his hips and grimacing with each breath. Jimmy slid down to the river to check on him and when Perona nodded something to him he splashed over in his cowboy boots to the scraggly root end of the tree that pinned me. He surveyed it for a moment and then dropped to his knees in the icy water to get his shoulder underneath a branch. He grabbed the tree under the water and put everything he had into lifting it. I felt the tree shift, not much, but just enough to work my foot out from behind the stump. I lowered myself gingerly from the branch that I was hanging onto. My foot hurt like hell but I could put my weight on it. I waved at Jimmy, who was already leading Perona out of the river. We looked like the survivors of a war, but we were alive.

We regrouped on the other side of the river. Perona moved slowly, holding his side. The horse was still shaking. Exhilarated by what I saw as my triumph over death and numbed by the excitement, I was bruised all over but still ready to lead the charge to Blue Lake. I felt the energy from the crystal in my knapsack urging me on. It wasn't until we discovered that Perona had broken several of his ribs that I realized we'd been defeated.

As the adrenaline wore off, the cold came stealing in. We rode back down the gorge for what seemed like hours until we came to a small clearing where we could build a fire. Perona collected moss from beneath the trees while Jimmy scouted around, breaking dry dead wood from the lower branches. Much to my surprise we soon had a roaring fire going and we sat steaming around it like baking potatoes, trading stories and tearing into the french bread and cheese I'd brought up from San Francisco, the only food we had.

I was concerned that our accident was some kind of omen. Jimmy and Perona shook their heads at the same time. They saw resistance as a positive sign, like the spring in a sapling. What we were doing was very important, they asserted. Otherwise, why had the Creator seen fit to test our resolve in this way?

Perona walked most of the ten miles back to Jimmy's ranch, claiming that he was starting to stiffen up. When we got there at eight o'clock it was raining and bitterly cold. There was no sign of Jimmy's girlfriend or his pickup truck. We turned the horses out and started to walk the three miles back to the Pueblo. Jimmy's girlfriend skidded up in a cloud of blue smoke a mile later.

I packed up quickly back at the trailer, wary of getting snowed in at Taos, said good-bye, closed the big door of my rented Lincoln and then I was instantly back in the world that I had left behind, a world that Jimmy and Perona had never known. I drove through Taos listening to soft music on the radio, while the heater clicked and whirred, and the wipers chased the huge flakes of snow back and forth across the windshield.

I had no idea what had gone wrong with my mission, or why it had nearly cost us our lives. I still don't know today. Perhaps the owl spirit, Hinhan Nagi, had found us wanting and hurled us down the mountain for our impetuousness. Sioux men wore secret spiritual tattoos on their wrists which were said to secure Hinhan's blessing as they journeyed to the Milky Way. All that I had was my determination. I knew that I would return to Blue Lake, until the time came when I heard that owl call my name if I had to, and I was taking that crystal with me.

∞ **11** ∞

The Owl's Blessing

A few months after my first trip to Blue Lake, I noticed that I was having trouble sleeping. I had started to hear a kind of a hum between my ears. I tried to ignore it at first, thinking that it might be some early sign of mental illness—the failure of my businesses was causing me no small amount of stress at the time. I tried playing music when I went to bed, a solution that my wife didn't appreciate and when that didn't work I tried unplugging my clock radio instead.

When I suggested that we try turning off the power at the meter my wife looked at me as if to say that clearly I was on the brink of insanity. Perhaps I was.

"You're right," I averred. "Let me just go look in there one more time." She rolled her eyes. I'd already treated her to the spectacle of me crawling around on all fours in my underwear pressing my ear to the walls and the furniture like a restless dog.

I sat on the bed like I'd seen TM people do and cleared my head of extraneous thoughts. Instantly the humming became louder. Clearly, if I was hearing the sound, I was also perceiving it on other levels. The more I focused on it, the louder it became. I opened my eyes after a few minutes, and walked straight to the glass display cabinet that held the crystal I'd nearly died for. The crystal itself was creating a kind of a low, pulsating hum. I reached for it, and then yanked my hand away in shock.

The crystal was hot.

I sat down on the bed to think about this for a moment. Unable to reach any firm conclusions, I retrieved a pair of gloves and a shovel from the garage, dug a shallow hole under a tree in my backyard, and buried the crystal, point downward. That took care of the infernal hum, but the crystal itself remained stubbornly lodged in my consciousness. I thought about it often, and at inappropriate times, like an old flame or a forbidden love. I wanted to get my mission over with so that I could think of something else, but there were still more obstacles to overcome.

In the first place, Blue Lake was still snowed in. The river route was nearly impassable at the best of times, and the only alternative was a 14,000 foot pass between two mountains. You couldn't get up there with a dog team. Then there was the fact that the War Council plainly didn't want me to go there. It was nothing personal: They didn't want anyone to go there who wasn't a member of the tribe. The Spirit of the North watched over the lake all winter but when the snows melted, armed guards took over. They stood watch all summer long, until the snows returned to relieve them, and they would shoot intruders on sight. The lake was guarded on other levels as well.

I had talked to Jimmy a few times over the winter, and he assured me that he was as gung-ho as ever to help me bring the crystal home to Blue Lake. So was Perona, but he was still mending from his experience as the Taos Pueblo's only human cannonball. We both believed that what we were doing was in accordance with the divine order and flow of things, and that a gateway would thus be opened for us, but that the timing could be crucial.

Late in the Summer of 1987, Jimmy finally called me. It was time. The entire Pueblo trekked to Blue Lake once

136

every year for one of their most important ceremonies. We would have a small window of opportunity just after they left. Jimmy had checked and the way was clear.

The flight to Albuquerque wouldn't have been fast enough for me if it was on the Concorde. I wanted to speed all of the way to Taos too, but I remembered the fireside discussion I'd had with Jimmy and Perona about resistance and listened to loud music instead. Soon the highway rose out of the desert like the back of a great stretching cat and I could feel the vibration change as I moved into the mountains. Santa Fe came and went and then I was in Taos, and thirty minutes after that I was seeing Jimmy's weathered mobile home growing large in my windshield. Jimmy shouldered the warped door open from inside like a police raid in reverse and we were two old friends again, trading war stories and our dreams of the future.

Jimmy told me about a friend of his, Fred Hopper, who in turn had told him about three shamans who'd come all the way from Mexico. The shamans, Jimmy said, had built a medicine wheel on the side of a hill overlooking the pueblo. Fred had been there, and had told Jimmy that it was a beautiful ceremony, that they'd all heard sounds and seen dancing lights over the crystals that the shamans had used. The purpose of the medicine wheel, the shamans had said, was to prepare for the arrival of a crystal. Jimmy lowered his head slightly to fix me with a significant look. I nodded. He hadn't told anyone about what we were doing but it seemed that somehow these old men who barely spoke English knew.

They all came around to the trailer that night. The shamans were delightful human beings, ageless and yet very old. They wore elaborately beaded buckskin robes, smiled often, and listened very carefully. I unwrapped the crystal and held it up to show them. The sunset spilling in through the windows made it look like I was holding a flame between my hands. The old shamans' eyes were as wide as saucers. This was the crystal, they explained to me in broken English. This was the reason that they'd traveled to the Pueblo. I could feel the crystal throbbing as I held it. It had brought all of us together. All of us had traveled thousands of miles thinking we were traveling alone, but we had been together the whole time.

My spirits fell a little bit when I checked my watch. I had planned to go into Taos that night to provision myself for the trip to Blue Lake. I'd heard stories about Jimmy's cooking and I didn't want to take any chances, but by the time that all of our guests left it was too late. Jimmy pushed his chair back and stretched. "Better check the grub," he said grinning.

I made a show of stretching and yawning, and then I slowly made my way into the kitchen. I found Jimmy staring into a steaming pot of what looked like swamp water. He stuck a big fork into the water, and then pulled out something like an enormous gray eel for my approval. I stared at it, trying not to look horrified. Jimmy dropped it back into the pot with a splash. He shook his head slowly, audibly sniffing the steam to show me how good it was. All he said was: "Beef tongue. Good."

My stomach drew itself up into a tight fist like a cornered porcupine. I thought about the bread and cheese I had planned to get in Taos, where it would have fit my knapsack, and what it would have been like to tear warm french bread apart at 14,000 feet. Obviously, I rationalized, the seriousness of my mission demanded that I fast.

We were up before dawn the next morning. Perona would only be with us in spirit this year, as would my Uncle Drunvalo. This time we began by following the river route, and then departed from it to climb to a steep pass at close to the 14,000 foot level. Even though it was a beautiful day, and the only snow we saw was at the very highest levels, I tried to stay as aware of my surroundings as possible, in case we encountered any more "resistance." Soon the juniper and pinyon pine gave way to quaking aspens which gave way to nothing at all as we climbed above the treeline and finally gained the saddle between mountains that divided up from down. Below us was Blue Lake, so far below that it appeared no bigger than a coffee cup, shining a beautiful iridescent blue as though it had been poured full of liquid turquoise.

The path down was so steep that we had to dismount and lead the horses. The lake slowly enlarged ahead of us and with it my anticipation grew. I was on the verge of completing something that all of us had risked our lives for, and it didn't appear that anything short of an earthquake could stop us now.

When we reached the lake, I was immediately struck by a massive flat-topped rock, which jutted out into the lake like a small island. It was the perfect place for us to perform a ceremony, and once we secured the horses I immediately started setting up on its broad surface. First I pulled out the crystal itself and carefully unwrapped it. Perona had made us a gift of feathers from all types of different birds, wrapped in corn husks, and Jimmy had wrapped all of the feathers and corn husks around the crystal. Over this he had tied a piece of leather with leather laces. I placed this beside the white buckskin pouch that my good friend Mary Schlosser, whose pueblo name is Cradle Flower, had given me. The pouch was filled with sacred corn meal, sacred because it was ground by virgins. I made a circle with various fetishes, Perona's feathers, other crystals, with the smoky mountain quartz from Clear Lake in the center. Then I sprinkled a pinch of the corn meal in each of the four directions in the way that Mary had taught me. After I had finished my ceremony, Jimmy sang traditional Pueblo songs and danced. We followed that with about an hour of prayer. After the prayer we looked at each other. It was time.

Jimmy stood out on the tip of the rock and I stood behind him with my hand on his left shoulder. The lake, which had been as smooth as glass when we started our ceremony, was now rippling. The ripples spread in broad circles from a central vortex. The hum that I'd heard back in my bedroom in Clear Lake, was audible again now, and growing steadily louder. Jimmy cocked his arm and threw the crystal. It arced over the water, catching the sun for a fleeting instant before falling directly into the center of the vortex.

Instantly, Jimmy and I were hit by a blast of energy that felt like a hurricane force wind. At the same time, I could feel a change in energy within me. It felt like I was being tuned up an octave, like a piano. I could feel the energy in my heart chakra move up to my throat chakra. I heard coughing behind me and spun around. Jimmy had fallen to the ground and was rolling and holding onto his throat. I made to move toward him but he waved me off. Whatever energy shift that I had felt, had triggered his asthma. I turned back to the lake. The ripples that we'd seen when we started were now small waves and the hum that I had heard was much louder. I decided, foolishly, to try and move the energy up even higher, to the level of the third eye. I knelt down and hummed a tone equal in frequency to the sound coming from the lake. Then I slowly raised the frequency upward.

The next think I knew I was lying on the ground next to Jimmy. As soon as I had tried to raise the pitch of the sound, I felt a sudden intense pain in my third eye. It felt just like someone had thrown a knife at me. I raised my head enough to look over to Jimmy. He looked at me from the corner of his eye and grinned as he gasped for air. We both looked as though we had just fallen off a train. I just lay there listening to the lake hum, feeling the good hot sun on my face, and listening to Jimmy trying to suck in enough of that rarefied mountain air to get his voice back.

Finally we both recovered to the point that we could pack up everything and head back. Jimmy said something about stopping to eat but to be honest I was kind of hoping that he'd forget—I could live without seeing him slice into a big cold gray beef tongue. Once we had gotten back over the pass, we turned off of the trail that we had taken coming in and followed a shallow creek to a clearing where the people from the pueblo camped on their visits to Blue Lake. Like a magician, Jimmy gestured to a a big green garbage bag, hanging from ropes between two trees. It was the pantry that the native people used to keep their food safe from animals. Jimmy unknotted the rope and lowered the garbage bag to the ground. Reaching inside it, he handed me a foil-wrapped package. Inside, I found a loaf of bread that his mother had baked the day before and a block of fresh cheese. I was ecstatic. It was exactly what I had wanted. As I tore into the bread I knew that despite all of the millions that I had lost I would never lack for anything again. The bread and cheese, forty miles from anywhere, was to me absolute proof of my powers of manifestation.

Jimmy and I wolfed down our lunch, giggling like two children drunk on mayhem. Something very big had just happened at Blue Lake. Unfortunately, neither of us had any idea what it was.

We followed the river back to Jimmy's ranch, instead of the steep trail that we had come in on. If anything, it seemed ever more overgrown after a season of winter storms than it had been when we tried to make our way up it the previous year. Nobody had been down it with a chainsaw in a long time. Blown-down trees were everywhere, necessitating constant detours. After about three hours of bushwhacking our way back down the mountain, we came to the spot where the accident had taken place the previous year. There, almost exactly over the rock where I had nearly been killed, I saw a big cow skull in the branch of a tree. Whether it had been there on our previous trip I couldn't say, but it looked like it had been there forever.

I stood up in the stirrups and tried to wrench it loose from the tree as I rode underneath but it wouldn't budge. The more I pulled, the more nervous my horse got. I looked down at the rock below us, let go of the skull, and rode on. Another lesson about letting go, I decided.

By about seven o'clock we had made our way back to the picnic ground where the trail widened out to a jeep trail about a mile away from the trailhead. It was at that point that I saw something that nearly made me fall off my horse. The trail was lined on both sides with the ghosts of hundreds of Native Americans. They stared up at Jimmy and me, their faces shining with joy and gratitude. I felt my own heart singing in resonance with them. I knew what we had done was big, and now I knew that it was really big, big enough for a parade even. My eyes brimmed with tears as we rode slowly past them. Both men and women were there and all of them were wearing ceremonial costumes. They looked up at me like I was somebody, like I had purpose in the world, like I wasn't the chalk outline of a man that I thought I had become.

In the ensuing years I would be given more and more information about what really happened at Blue Lake that day. The first big piece came only two months later. As part of my hypnotherapy training, I had a session with Bill Baldwin where I asked to look at the most evil lifetime that I had ever had on earth. In this session, described in a later chapter, I would learn enough of my own history, and the history of the crystal to understand why I felt so driven to put things right.

The final piece of information came on my last visit to Taos. For several years residents of Taos have complained about a mysterious hum. A congressional inquiry, and a number of scientific investigations later, the "Taos Hum," as the newspapers have dubbed it, continues to frustrate residents. I looked Jimmy up in August of 1995 and our conversation turned to the subject of the noise that everyone seems to be able to hear but that no one has ever been able to record.

"You know what it is, don't you Ken?" Jimmy said significantly.

I thought about it for a moment. Then I looked at him. Hard.

"It's the same noise, right?" he said. I nodded slowly. He was right. It was. Exactly.

∞ **12** ∞

The Dolphin Swimmer

In 1994, I gave a workshop in Bellevue, Washington. Tom was a psychologist who had come to my workshop and then signed up for a session with me afterwards. He brought his wife along. She was going to wait out by the motel swimming pool while I worked on her husband. Tom's wife was a heavyset woman, obviously well-off, and obviously very skeptical of what her husband had told her about me. Her husband by comparison was as excited about his session as a puppy about to go for a walk. He couldn't wait to experience some of the things that he'd seen my clients experience in my workshop.

Ninety minutes later, which is when I normally end my sessions, Tom was still on the table, and still raring to go. I had taken care of all of his soul fragments, energies, and entities, but when it came to the past lives that he needed to look at to make sense of his life today, Tom had suddenly gone holographic on me. He was racing through thirty simultaneous past lives like someone on a paid shopping spree at Bloomingdale's. I listened in awe. Meanwhile, his wife paced back and forth metronomically in her fur coat out by the pool like a polar bear at the zoo. Sensing her mounting irritation, I poked my head out of the motel room door. Her husband lay babbling ecstatically about Egypt on my massage table behind me.

"He's just looking at some past lives," I explained apologetically. She raised her eyebrows in a clear expression of disapproval as she brushed past me to see for herself what state her husband was in.

"I want to be sick now," her husband chimed in from the table, in the middle of one of his past life recollections.

I hurried back over to the table. "No you don't," I said firmly. This worked almost every time. I didn't like having clients throw up around me. If I liked that sort of thing I would have become a nurse.

"No," said the husband. "You don't understand. I really want to be sick." His emphasis on the word want was meant to convey that this was a necessary part of his spiritual experience. Maybe he was remembering a peyote initiation.

His wife looked at me expectantly. I sighed. "Okay," I told him. "If you absolutely have to be sick, go use the bathroom, okay?"

"Okay!" he chirped happily. He leapt up and ran into the bathroom, practically bouncing off of the walls as he went. His wife by way of contrast, stood staring at me like I was a museum curiosity. The bathroom door slammed. A moment later we heard the unmistakable sound of the toilet lid being flipped up, followed by the equally unmistakable sound of one ecstatic psychologist yelling "BUUU-ICK!" into a porcelain bullhorn. There was nothing that I could say to his wife at this point. She rolled her eyes skyward and sighed as her husband serenaded us. Finally the toilet flushed and it was quiet again.

By then I'd succeeded in engaging the psychologist's wife in an awkward conversation. Things were looking up, or so I thought. Her husband had other ideas. He started to serenade us again. This time it sounded like someone trying to sing underwater. "Bloobloobloo-blooblooo-aaah!" he yelled. I smiled weakly at the psychologist's wife and excused myself.

When I opened the bathroom door, the psychologist was still on his knees in front of the toilet. He had loosened his tie and draped it over one shoulder. His head was in the bowl and he was blowing bubbles. Weird! I thought to myself.

"What are you doing?" I asked him. He didn't hear me right away.

"Bloob-bloob-bloog-aaah!" he repeated.

"What are you doing?" I asked him again.

He paused to suck air between bubbles. "I'm bloob-bloob-bloob swimming with the dolphins!" he bubbled excitedly. That was all I needed to hear. I backed out of the bathroom and carefully shut the door. His wife waited for me with arms folded.

"He's, uh, swimming with the dolphins," I told her. She looked at me like I was the one with my head in the toilet. I shrugged. "Maybe you should wait outside for a few minutes," She considered this. The sound of her husband blowing bubbles in the toilet filled the space between us like muzak for the criminally insane.

"Maybe I'd better," she said.

When Tom finally emerged from the bathroom, he had a glow about him and a serenity that I hadn't seen before. He looked at me with either tears or toilet water in his eyes. "Nothing like this has ever happened to me before," he told me sincerely. We stood looking at each other for a long time, like two brothers. "Thank you," he said finally.

Months later, I got a letter from Tom that detailed how his experience had changed his life. No one had been able to work with him before. After our visit, he saw himself and his work in a completely different way. He had decided to renew his study of psychology, only instead of going back to the university, he was going to study with the Native Americans who lived in the Seattle area. I felt very blessed for meeting him. I'd always known that there was a sacred power imminent in all things, that God was everywhere, but the truth of this was never quite so clear as it was on the day when I saw someone find enlightenment in a toilet.

∞ **13** ∞

Gor

I believe that we have learned as much from darkness as we have from light. Living, as we have been, in a polarity-based universe there is no alternative. Knowing this means facing the reality that, somewhere in all of our thousands of lifetimes in this universe, we have embodied evil ourselves in order to learn from it.

Understanding this, that we are not perfect, and that all of us have embodied evil at one time or another, is a very important lesson for anyone who chooses a career in the healing arts. Without this knowledge, it is all too easy to find ourselves in the position of judging our clients for what we see as the evils that they have committed. Seeing the darkest side of ourselves, is part of the process of fully accepting our humanity. I know this now, and I owe this knowledge to an extraordinary session I had when I was a student of Bill Baldwin's.

I lay back in a chair in Bill Baldwin's classroom. We were there to try to divine the truth of the crystal that I had nearly died trying to take to Blue Lake. In my quest for this truth, I would find myself reliving a lifetime in which I had been someone or something more evil that I would have ever previously imagined. Bill carefully led me into an altered state. The room was filled with my fellow students who were arrayed on pillows. They had come to watch my session as I had watched so many of theirs. A video camera on a tripod recorded everything, without judgment. The day was November 1, 1987, All Saints Day. Soon, I forgot all about the classroom, the camera, and the people watching me. I was in another world.

I was a twelve year old boy living in a pre-industrial society in Turkey. My parents were poor and cursed my very existence for the bread that I took from their mouths. Only the tattered remnants of their religious beliefs stopped them from killing me. Instead they beat me, and starved me, in the hope that I would die of more natural causes. I limped around the village in rags, my legs bowed from rickets. Other children laughed and stoned me. I decided that I wouldn't give anyone the satisfaction of seeing me die. Instead, I ran away one night to the acrid hills that overlooked the town. I had no intention other than escape, and no food or water beyond what little I carried in my stomach. Within two days, the sun had nearly driven all of the life out of me. I didn't care. Anything was better than the existence I had been living. I hated my parents for what they'd done to me, and hated the entire village for not helping me.

I stumbled from rock to rock like a drunken man, dizzy and delirious from dehydration. I kept moving higher rather than lower, wanting to die as far away from the village as I could. A black shape loomed ahead of me like a painted shadow. As I approached I could feel a seductive cool breeze. Then the blackness swallowed me completely.

I awoke on the cool stone floor of a cave the next morning feeling strangely refreshed, as though I'd taken a step backwards from the brink of death. The pounding headache and dizziness that were the signatures of my dehydration were both gone. Instead, I felt curiously light-headed and clear. Behind me I could see the sun pounding down on the overexposed rocks like a blacksmith's hammer. I turned inward, toward the cave's dimly lit interior.

Something glowed faintly in the cavern ahead of me, with a dim gray-green phosphorescence that seemed to go right through me, like radiation. My heart quickened as I drew closer. There, lying on the ground in front of me was a crystal, the same smoky mountain quartz crystal that one day in another lifetime I would nearly die trying to take to Blue Lake. I reached for it greedily, feeling a strange roaring sound between my ears. The crystal was small enough to hold in my hands, and as I held it, I felt the energy, the radiation coursing through my nervous system, jumping from synapse to synapse until I felt like I was vibrating. At that moment the crystal and I became each other, and at that moment I realized my destiny, as surely as if I had just pulled a sword from a stone. I had made a bargain.

I grew stronger every day, nourished by the energy inside the crystal, and as I grew stronger I thought of revenge against the people of my village. I thought of my father, who had whipped and beaten me like a dog, and my mother, who had let him. I thought of the other children who stoned me whenever they saw me outside of my hovel. I thought of all of the people who could have helped me and didn't. I hated them all, and the more I hated the stronger the crystal's vibration seemed to become, the energy cycling back and forth between us until I realized that my hate was now becoming power. With the power came a new name: Gor.

I decided to stop the rain. They would learn the pain of slow starvation firsthand, just as they had taught it to me. Although I never left the cave, I could see everything. I watched the crops in the fields shrivel up and die, saw the wind carry the precious soil away, and when everything else was gone I saw the farmers fall upon their precious oxen like wolves.

After a while, manipulating the weather wasn't enough for me. The cave was gone, replaced by an immense dark castle that the crystal had helped me to make real. The more power I had, the more energy I seemed to need. I decided that I wanted to destroy everything. I took the vibration of hate and fear that people were sending me, condensed it, and inserted it into the body of a flea. The flea would reproduce, the rats would carry the fleas into the houses and then all would be devastation. Knowing all of these things, I sent the rat into the city and sat down in my castle to wait. I had created the black plague.

As bubonic plague spread across Europe, borne on the backs of rats, the energy of death and pain came back to me in waves. Each wave lifted me higher, raising my energy level. The sensation was very pleasurable. I sat in a chair in my castle, drinking in the energy of pain and suffering, like a satyr. I set up a kind of oscillation, pushing each wave out so that it would come back harder and faster. The more people that died, the better I felt. Toward the end, when hundreds of thousands of people were dying every day, it was like that feeling you get on a swing as a child, when you think you're going to vault clear over the crossbar.

Then, as calculating as I was, I somehow lost control. I felt the energy coming in toward me like a tidal wave. There was no way I could push it back out again. Before I could even open my mouth to scream, it hit me. I felt myself imploding, falling into myself like a black hole, into nothingness.

The next thing that I knew, I was an enormous barnacled whale swimming in an immense blue ocean. I was on another planet, one completely covered by water. It was my home, where I'd come from before I had ever been human in the first place. The calmness I felt was almost indescribable. Everything was oneness. I could sense no boundaries, no differences between me and any other thing. The water was as much as part of me as my skin, as were the barnacles, and all of the other whales. We were all one. Whatever I thought, encompassed me. My thoughts weren't just inside my head like they are when you're in human form. As a whale, every thought that I had, instantly became part of the whale consciousness, part of my reality, part of me, part of everything.

∞ **14** ∞

Kauai

I didn't begin my life believing in miracles. Although my mother was a twelfth degree Rosicrucian, it was my father's and my stepfather's more pragmatic beliefs that were the first to rub off on me. They believed that we made our own miracles through hard work, and that was the path that I followed until finally the rains came and took it all away from me. From that time on I was open to miracles of any kind. At first it was my increasing desperation over my seeming inability to change my world through any other means that drove me toward prayer. As years went by, and I finally found peace with what I had lost, I began to understand that miracles had always been part of my life, and then I began to see them everywhere.

Miracles and wedding cakes both have to be made of something. A wedding cake might begin with a baker gazing at a sack of flour, and out of that subtle communication, like lovers whose glances cross for the first time, earth, water, air and fire would all be called forth to join together in the magic dance of creation. Before there were diamonds and pearls, there first had to be coal and sand, all the way back to the very first miracle, that was made up of nothing at all.

I didn't have much more than coal and sand in 1989, when I found myself in Bellingham, Washington, standing with my hands in my pockets and staring up at the red brick facade of a restored nineteenth century building. I wasn't thinking much about miracles that day. If I allowed myself to dwell on anything, it was my troubles with my relationships and the endless machinations associated with my four bankruptcies.

Still, I kept staring up at the third floor of the building, and at the sign that hung out front which read "The Black Cat." I was quite superstitious in those days, having begun my dealings with satanic cults and witchcraft, and so it was a little hard for me to walk up three flights of stairs to visit a cramped little antique store with a name like that. Finally the pull of whatever was in that store defeated my remnants of common sense and up I went.

As I wandered about the store, the rough pine boards creaking under my feet, I found myself irresistibly drawn to an old oak curio cabinet, something like the one that I used to hide my chocolate bars in when I was five. I pressed my nose to the dusty glass. A large cherry amethyst crystal winked at me as my shadow crossed over it. I turned around to see the storekeeper watching me intently. "Go ahead," he said, encouragingly. "Take a look."

I carefully opened the doors of the cabinet, lifted the crystal off its pewter stand and held it up against one of the store's windows. It trapped the sunlight like blood holds the essence of life. I could feel that it had a power, a power that had something to do with light. Then I gasped. There, carved on its face was a beautiful and intricate image of an elephant's head. I hadn't ever seen anything like it.

"Nice, huh," said the storekeeper, interrupting my reverie. I nodded slowly, wistfully replacing the crystal in the cabinet. Unfortunately, I wasn't a millionaire any longer, and at $450 the crystal wasn't exactly priced to move. I thanked the store owner and left with the unpleasant impotent feeling born of having once had the experience of being able to buy almost anything that I wanted.

Ten minutes before the store closed for the day, I was back. I was supposed to be in Bellingham on business but all that I had been able to think about for the rest of that day was the fiery cherry amethyst crystal. My higher self had been broadcasting the same message over and over. The message was, "buy the crystal." I tried to work some of the old Ken Page king of the salesmen magic by talking the storekeeper down, but he wouldn't budge. "We take credit cards," he said with finality. The bidding was closed.

I took the crystal back with me to my hotel room at the Rodeway Inn. The next evening I carried it down to the hotel's hot tub with me, and held it to my forehead. I learned several things. The crystal belonged somewhere on the island of Kauai, I was to take it there, and taking it there would somehow alter the earth's grids. My trip to Kauai would cost me nothing, but there was no information as to when this trip would materialize. Then, as soon as I lowered the crystal from my forehead, I had an emotional breakdown. Much later I would realize that this, like my trip, was a gift that far outstripped the money that I had spent on the crystal.

From that time on, I carried that crystal with me like a religious talisman, never knowing when I would be called upon to pick up and leave for the Hawaiian Islands. Nearly a year later, in March of 1990, the trip finally materialized. As the crystal had told me, the trip would cost me no money, although like all of my adventures it would require some commerce in emotions.

The trip was the brainchild of a friend of mine named Rose who wanted to take me along on her vacation. She was going to Kauai to visit two of her friends, both of whom I knew as well. Knowing that there was a higher purpose involved, I had no trouble in accepting her offer.

I'd first met Rose years before when she sponsored my work in Southern California. Her husband was a multi-millionaire, and they allowed me to see my clients in their house, giving me the use of a beautiful room with stained glass windows and an entire wall painted with angels.

Rose's husband died about two years after I had met her. Two months after his funeral, which I attended, and a few days into the first Christmas holiday that I had ever spent alone, I gave Rose a call. Her situation was the same. She invited me down to spend the next several days and New Year's eve in Palm Springs with her. She didn't have to ask me twice. Anything was better than spending another moment of the holidays alone in my motor home.

On the third day of my visit, Rose came into my room and sat on my bed. She had something important to tell me. Her wealth had become a burden to her. She continued, "I want to give you all of my money," I blinked.

"I don't want your money, sweetheart," I replied carefully. She told me that if I didn't take her money she would give it to a religious commune. I had visited the commune with her and seen enough to know that her money would not be spent wisely there. She even told me that one of the commune's "priestesses" had asked for her three caret diamond ring, claiming that it held Rose's vibration. I agreed to take her money, knowing that I would only be holding it for her until she was ready to take it herself.

I was king for a day. Rose told me that I now had a monthly income of $17,000, her house, and my pick of a fleet of cars. All that she wanted was a single room. The gift was largely symbolic; we had signed no papers and I left the Rolls Royce behind in her garage when I flew back to Oakland. Her bequest was never mentioned again.

Rose invited me to Kauai a few months later. It was on my way there, as the plane floated above a downy pillow of clouds, that I received another one of the messages that periodically turned my life upside down. "Your work on earth is done," a voice told me, "and, you can leave if you wish." I was offered a balance sheet and a one-way ticket to other realms. According to the balance sheet, I had so far helped to heal thousands of people, balanced negativity all over the planet, and helped millions of lost souls return to the light. If I stayed, I was told, I would assist millions more lost souls and help to change earth as I knew it. If I left, I would become a teacher of guides and angels on other levels. As I was already seeing the destruction of all of my businesses, my family and my relationships, the option of leaving sounded very attractive to me. I was even given a window of time in which to leave, the 17th, 18th, and 19th of March, 1991.

I could feel the presence of the cherry amethyst crystal in my pocket. I had a mission to complete, and for the moment, Rose and I were in love. I decided to hold my focus, stick around and see what would happen next.

The day after I got to Kauai, Rose and I had lunch with two friends of hers, one of whom was Lynn McFarlane, who was one of my very first students. We talked for a while after we ate, until I took advantage of a hiatus in the discussion to step outside onto the wooden deck that overlooked a backyard full of vibrant trees and flowers. It had rained while we were talking and the afternoon sun beamed down on all of the freshly washed foliage, highlighting every leaf and blade of grass as though it had just been painted. I soon found myself staring at an intricate spider's web. Backlit by the sun, and covered with tiny drops of water that shone like gemstones, it seemed to me at that moment to be one of the most overwhelmingly beautiful things that I had ever seen. Then, as my attention shifted to the architect of the web, the large dark spider in its center, something strange and miraculous happened. The spider began to talk to me.

I heard the voice of the spider inside my head, the same way that a person might remember a conversation. The spider's voice was neither male nor female, at least not in the way that I would have expected, although it did have a feminine seductive quality to it. It lectured to me for nearly thirty minutes. First of all the spider told me all about spells and witchcraft, and gave me the precise information that I could use to break any spell. Then it lectured me about the human nervous system, how it is affected or changed by every single thing that has ever happened to us, and how I could help to heal it.

The conversation ended as quickly as it had begun and then I was once again sitting on the deck, surrounded by flowers, staring up at the now silent and enigmatic spider with newfound respect and awe. By that time in my life, my reality had shifted so dramatically so many times that I didn't have any problems believing in talking spiders.

I spent the rest of my free time exploring the island's canyons, mountains and beaches, carrying the crystal with me all the while, hoping that I would be shown where it needed to go. I had some interesting adventures along the way. One of these began with a road sign, a gust of wind and a sharp curve in the road.

The sign was just as ordinary as the spider had been, the familiar standardized shape warning of a bend in the road ahead. One of the bolts that secured the sign to its post had come loose and a stiff breeze now animated the arrow, swinging it back and forth so that it pointed over and over, not at the curve but at something beyond the opposite shoulder. I slowed down to stare at it as I passed, and then a few hundred yards down the road I pulled over and stopped. I could see a small garden of pale white headstones over my left shoulder. I watched the sign swinging back and forth in my rear view mirror. It was pointing directly at the graveyard.

The cemetery was completely deserted. I wandered it like the tourist that I was, studying the lacquered photographs that were permanently attached to the head-stones, and reading the inscriptions beneath them. The markers offered no clues as to why I had been drawn to such a quiet and desolate place in the middle of a sunny afternoon. I listened carefully with my other senses as well, but all that I picked up was the vibration of a small child, who for some reason had been afraid to go into the light, and was waiting over the remains of her physical body for someone to show her the way home. At almost the same moment, I noticed for the first time the tall statue of Jesus that presided over a grassy and largely unused part of the cemetery. I walked toward it, but before I could get within twenty feet something started to happen. Something wonderful.

The ground shook beneath my grass-stained sneakers like an earthquake. I could hear a roaring sound, like something between a jet engine and a hurricane, steadily increasing in volume. I stopped in my tracks, standing as still as though my feet had been nailed to the ground. Then the unseen energy that was building beneath me exploded, surging upward like an enormous volcanic erup-tion. I could sense the souls of the dead flying past me like bits of straw in a hurricane, flying straight upward, drawn by a force so immensely powerful that there was no gravity in the universe to rival it. I know now that force was love. I could only sense the souls racing by me for a tiny fraction of an instant, but in that moment I could briefly feel their essence. It was like listening to all of the long-distance phone calls in the world at once. I stood there in awe and confusion, holding my arms out from my sides, staring at the statue of Jesus, doing my best to be with whatever it was that was happening. It seemed to go on forever, for five, ten minutes or longer.

When it finally stopped, my legs buckled and I sat down hard on the ground. Everything was completely still. The birds, the insects, even the wind were all at prayer together, as was I. It was the stillness borne of complete balance, a stillness that said God had just passed by.

I had physically become the vibration of the gateway between worlds for the first time. As I had become that gateway, the souls then had to pass through my vibration to go home, so that the energy I felt was actually moving through me. This, I realized was the truth of what it meant to be a gatekeeper, to actually become the gate. Being a gatekeeper also had to do with the control of time, for the gate had to exist somehow outside of time, or at least outside of the linear tabulated time of the three dimensional world.

Earlier that morning, March 19th, I had made the decision to stay on earth. I decided that I didn't understand relationships, and that I wanted to learn everything about them. Instantly, I heard a voice booming in my head like thunder. The voice said, "Congratulations, you've gotten it! By the way," it added, "you are now a Gatekeeper." My experience in the cemetery was designed to teach me exactly what that meant.

Although thousands and thousands of trapped souls had just found their way home, I still had one homeless crystal to deal with. I'd carried that crystal thousands of miles, from Washington to California and across the Pacific to Hawaii, a journey that might have taken one of

160

the ancients their entire life to accomplish, and I still had no idea what I was supposed to do with it. After I'd visited all of the special places that the tourist guides talked about and drawn a blank, I decided to call my friend Katrina Raphael, who was living on Kauai at the time and knew more about crystals than just about anybody.

Katrina told me about the Crystal Lingam Iraivan Temple, located on the sacred Wailua River in Kapaa. When I learned that the world's largest natural quartz crystal was enshrined there, I knew I had to visit.

The temple itself was a beautiful building, entirely constructed of stone, hand-carved in India and shipped by freighter to Kauai. It was surrounded on all sides by carefully tended pools and gardens. I didn't know it when I arrived, but the temple was only open to the public at specified times, and I hadn't arrived during one of them. Nevertheless, I stood peering hopefully through the doorway until finally one of the orange-robed priests saw me and invited me in. The temple's central altar was dominated by the massive, 700 pound earthkeeper crystal, flanked on either side by statues of Ganesha, the elephant god known as the remover of obstacles.

The priest inclined his head, beckoning me to follow. The service was already under way in an adjoining room. I sat down on the right side with the men. Although the puja they were performing was entirely unfamiliar to me, I was able to follow along and I alternated between carefully watching my neighbors to see what I was to do next and staring at the massive six-sided crystal in the next room.

I knew almost as soon as I saw the great earthkeeper crystal that the cherry amethyst that I had bought nearly a year ago in Bellingham, Washington belonged here in a Hindu temple on Kauai. After the service, I spoke to one of the priests and told him why I had come. I showed him the cherry amethyst, and explained that it belonged on the face of the earthkeeper crystal. It was the earthkeeper's eye. Opening my hand dramatically I said: "This is the most valuable thing that I own. I have been instructed to give it to your head priest." The priest I was talking to frowned and shook his head doubtfully. He said that what I was asking would be most difficult. The head priest rarely came into the temple at all, and spoke to visitors even more rarely. "Nevertheless," I told him, "I will be back in two days, at eleven o'clock, to present this crystal to your order and I would be honored if the head priest would be here to receive it."

Two days later, Rose and I returned as promised to the Hindu temple and knelt down not far from the huge crystal. I noticed that in addition to the white-robed acolytes, there were more of the orange-robed priests than I had seen the first time that I was there. I craned my head and looked around. There were five of them, each standing at a different station in the temple. A moment later everyone in the temple was prostrating themselves, lying flat on their stomachs on the floor. The head priest had entered. He smiled at all of us as he walked lightly to the altar where the crystal presided.

"Do you mind if I sit down for a moment?" he asked cheerfully. No one said anything. I could tell from looking at the white-robed devotees that several of them had never been this close to their spiritual leader before. He smiled at each of us as he sat down. Although he appeared to be in his fifties, his eyes sparkled like a child's. "Now then," he said, taking us all in. "Does anyone have anything to share?"

My hand shot up. "I do," I said. He nodded, still smiling. "May I approach you?"

"By all means," the priest replied, beckoning me to do so. I held out the crystal as I neared him.

162

"This is the eye of the earthkeeper crystal," I explained carefully. "It is the most valuable thing that I own and I want to give it to you."

He held the crystal up to the light like a jeweler, turning it slowly first one way and then another. Finally he nodded. "How did you come to be this way?" he asked.

I thought carefully before I answered. "I have been looking inside myself for a long time," I replied honestly.

The old yogi gestured toward all of his orange-robed priests, bidding them to pay attention. "This is what it looks like," he lectured them. "This is what it feels like. This is how you will recognize it, how it will appear to you."

I stiffened as he said these things. Slowly, I realized from the way that the priests were studying me that I was what he was talking about. I felt very honored.

"Well," the old man said pleasantly, "I must go to India soon." He talked a little about India and his mission there. He was going to supervise the stonecutters who were cutting stone to be shipped back to Hawaii for their new temple. When he concluded his story, he looked directly at me and said "Thank you." Then he left.

Rose and I looked at each other. I could see that she was now looking at me in the way that the priests had, trying to gauge for herself exactly what it was that the old man had seen in me. Although I don't think she saw what the priest had seen, I could tell that my stock with her had risen considerably. She kept studying me on the way home and was somehow moved by the events of the day to tell me that she had had the most profound experience of her life the day before. I leaned forward in my seat, waiting for her explanation. "But I can't tell you about it," she said sadly. "Sorry."

I sighed. It felt like she was talking about some kind of relationship problem. I preferred not to mix my great spiritual experiences with my great unresolved issues, although I realized that the two were probably in some way inseparable.

"And," Rose went on, "I've scheduled a massage for you tomorrow." Her words dripped with hidden import. She made it sound like scheduling a massage for me was the most profound experience of her life. I couldn't see the connection. I thanked her and told her that a massage sounded great.

The next morning Rose dropped me off at a shack on the edge of a beautiful white beach. "Have a great massage," she said, her words still pregnant with hidden meaning. I watched her drive off, wondering if I would ever really understand her.

I knocked at the door of the shack. The door swung open. I stood on the threshold, blinking in surprise. The masseuse looked enough like Rose to be her sister. The only real physical difference between them was that the massage therapist was ten years younger. I had learned in my work as a healer that coincidences like this were seldom completely innocent, but I didn't have a clue as to what this one meant.

I was lying on my stomach staring out at the ocean through the shack's open french doors and having a wonderful time, when the masseuse suddenly lifted her hands from my back and said, "I can't work on you any more."

I propped myself up on one elbow to regard her. "What?" I asked. We were only forty five minutes into a two hour massage.

"I can't work on you anymore. There's something evil in here, something terribly evil and it's scaring me."

Evil, I thought to myself. I felt like Batman might have felt if his pager had gone off at Club Med. "Well," I sighed, "if you can peel me off of this table maybe I can help you. This is kind of what I do for a living."

I sat up with the sheet wrapped around me and tried to make contact with whatever it was that had interrupted my massage. The masseuse was too frightened to let me work with her directly, and so I assumed the role of trance medium myself. I felt the familiar weight around my head that was the empathic signature of a powerful energy. When I asked it what it was doing around my masseuse, it told me that it wanted to kill her.

"Kill her?" I said. Part of me wondered why it couldn't have waited until I had finished my massage to bring all of this up. "Why do you want to kill this woman?"

"Because we hate her!" the energy roared. So much for introductions. The trouble apparently had started when the masseuse and a friend had dug some holes for fence posts on one side of the property. In the process they had accidentally unearthed the bleached bones of the ancient Kahunas who had died in the very spot. The energy that I was talking to was what had killed them. Unearthing the bones had somehow drawn it back to the property, the site of one of its great battles. When the energy had finished its tale, I shifted it and sent it home. I used something I called the double pyramid release to draw all of the related energy from anywhere else on the planet that it was affecting. By the time all of that was completed, my appointment was over and Rose was pulling up outside. The masseuse thanked me profusely, and begged me to come back the next day to finish my appointment. I readily agreed and on that note we parted.

The next morning when Rose asked me what I was planning to do with my day, I reminded her of my return engagement with the massage therapist. She had a lot of questions for me about it, questions that didn't make a whole lot of sense in light of the fact that she had made the appointment for me in the first place. "You're acting jealous," I told her flatly.

Her eyes welled up with tears. "Don't go," she implored. "If you go I'll lose you."

"Rose, what's going on here?" I demanded.

"Well," she sighed. "I suppose I had better tell you. I had a vision." I put down my coffee cup and listened. Her vision had come during her massage with the same masseuse. This was the most profound experience of her life, the one that for some reason she couldn't tell me about earlier. In her vision she saw Jesus standing before her, arrayed in brilliantly glowing robes. Jesus had spoken to her. He told Rose that I belonged in a relationship with the masseuse, not with her, and it was her duty to bring the two of us together. This was why Rose had made an appointment for me, to fulfill her "vision."

I told Rose that I needed some time alone and went out to sit on the balcony. I stared out at the peaceful blue Pacific, but I did not feel peaceful. I was seething. After a while Rose slipped through the sliding doors to ask me if I was all right. I told her I wasn't. I wasn't all right because she had sent me into a situation where I could have been killed. She hadn't seen Jesus, she had seen the energy that had killed the Kahunas. It looked like Jesus to her because she wanted it to, but it was a set-up. The energy's immediate purpose would have been to take me out. If she had shared with me, instead of believing that she knew enough to act in my greater good, I might not have walked blindly into such a potentially dangerous situation.

I knew that our relationship was essentially over. Rose was comfortable with her money again, and confident enough about herself that she was becoming increasingly critical of me. My mission on Kauai was nearly over as well and when it ended, I would sever all of my ties to Rose. Her money had never been mine to begin with, and now her life was her own as well.

The following day, which was Sunday, services at the temple were open to the public, and I went there with my friend Katrina Raphael. This time the temple filled near to capacity with forty or fifty people. My heart leaped when I looked over to the shrine where the giant earthkeeper crystal was. A thin gold wire ran around it, securing the cherry amethyst crystal to its face. I felt a small flush of pride. The cherry amethyst was in exactly the right place.

Halfway through the service, I heard a voice inside my head saying, "We need you to let go of your nervous system." My immediate response was far from positive. I had been asked to do so much already; this was too much. I had people all around me. What would happen if I let go of my nervous system? I knew what happened when people let go when they died. They made a big mess, that's what happened. After a short while I calmed down, realizing that I probably wouldn't be asked to lose control of myself in such a way in a sacred temple. I centered myself, and made the decision to do as the voice asked.

I looked over to the crystal. Instantly I felt myself being bombarded with a wave of energy. The waves kept coming faster and faster, just like they had at Blue Lake, only at a much greater frequency. I started to shake uncontrollably, like one of those wooden puppets that puppeteers bounce on their knees. Great, I thought to myself. I'm going to have some kind of seizure in a temple during Sunday services. How embarrassing.

Then it hit me. The shaking and the acceleration of the waves of energy were happening because I was hanging onto my nervous system. I needed to let it go completely. As soon as I let go completely I felt the cherry amethyst crystal on the face of the earth-keeper connect directly with my third eye. It was like I had picked up a fallen high tension wire and held it to my forehead. I felt a physical jolt and then I felt information pouring into me. The information was all about the nervous system, how to heal, how the body's energetic templates worked on other dimensional levels. The images flooded into my consciousness more quickly than I could ever hope to catalogue them. It was like a car mechanic being given all of the electrical information about every car in the world all at the same time, only I was learning how to heal the human nervous system. Just as suddenly as it started, the flood of energy stopped, leaving me with a sensation of being filled with a quiet, gentle power. I stared at the two crystals I had brought together. They had been forever changed by their association and so had I. I felt like I had died and been reborn, and I knew that I no longer needed to physically die. I felt like the shape of my head had changed, like the back of my skull extended outwards, like the ancient Egyptians, or the being that I had once recognized as another aspect of myself on a mortally wounded starship.

Immediately after the service, as I stood blinking and swaying in the bright sunlight outside the temple, wondering what on earth I was being prepared to do next, I heard a voice beside me. "Ken?" it said. I looked down to see my old friend Katrina Raphael. "I know that you're on vacation and everything, but I was wondering if you might do some work with me before you left. I've been feeling under the weather." She had been one of my first teachers about crystals and we had worked together several times before. I readily agreed.

We met at her house and as we sat together in her unfurnished living room she said, "God, I wish you could do something about my nervous system. I feel like it's totally fried." A light went on in my head.

"Well," I replied laconically, trying not to sound overly eager, "I've just been told how to work with the human nervous system. If you don't mind being the first-"

"I'm always the first!" she interrupted. "I'm always the one that gets sacrificed." She wasn't being facetious. I'd heard her relate the stories of some of her past lives. She had been sacrificed, many times. Most people I've met like Katrina, who have volunteered to come here as light-workers, have had some very unfortunate experiences in their past lives as a result of their spiritual vocation.

"Not this time," I said smiling.

Once we began the session together, it quickly became clear that her nervous system was in a very fragile state. She had channeled the bulk of the information in the three books that she had written and the energies that she had allowed to flow through her had damaged her nervous system. I had been instructed in exactly what to do by the spider. I silently uttered a brief prayer and bent down to touch my forehead to hers, allowing her to feel my female template so that she could rebuild her own.

The operation was a success. I rejoiced in the knowledge that I now had a whole new set of techniques to work with, and thought excitedly about all of the new clients and information my newfound knowledge would bring to me. My optimism was not in sync however with divine timing, and I went home to California to see my flow of clients slow to a trickle and then dry up entirely.

The truth was that in 1991, I was still so deeply enmeshed in the world of polarities that my knowledge of the nervous system and energetic templates made me as dangerous as a ten year old at the rudder of an oil tanker. My knowing about templates gave me the power to change things, based on my beliefs, and the state of evolution of my beliefs suggested that the changes I might make could hurt people.

Two months after I left Kauai I was living at my aunt's stables in my motorhome and feeling more sorry for myself than I ever have before or since. I would have no practice to speak of for more than a year, until I had learned enough to be safe again. Within months of finally learning my lessons about polarity consciousness, I would meet my wife Mary, and I would know then that the angels were still with me.

I met Mary when I offered to scan her horse for her. I knew that the two of them had gone over an embankment, and that both of them had been injured. She looked at me as though I were crazy, but she told me to go ahead. I stood beside the horse and ran my hands over it. I told her the history of its injuries. Then I moved my hands to the horse's head and told Mary about the thought form that I found there. The horse was afraid that it would be injured again and this fear was making the horse difficult to ride.

I looked over to Mary. Her look had changed from skepticism to astonishment and awe. I told her that I could do a past-life regression with her and her horse so that she could discover the truth of their lives together. When she told me that she also had migraine headaches, I bet her $20 that I could completely cure them during the same session.

Three days later, Mary, her horse, my cousin Cathy, and I, all stood in the horse's stall together. Cathy held the horse's reins. Mary stood with one hand on her horse and I stood beside her. Within moments, she was experiencing a past life where she and her horse both fell, and Mary's neck was broken. This was the pattern that they were giving energy to in their present life. Looking at her accident and understanding it fully for the first time, freed her from the need to subconsciously recreate the pain associated with the original injury. Mary's migraines disappeared, never to recur. I still have her $20.

Not long afterwards, we fell in love. When I left California, she came with me and together we set sail in my motorhome to co-create a new life together. Our physical journey ended in Texas where our spiritual journey has only just begun.

Soon after I met Mary, I met my partner Shirley Holly, and soon after that we were offered our own healing center in Houston. Within a year I would be giving workshops around the country. My mission to teach would eventually bring me to Montauk, Long Island, where I would use the knowledge that been given to me on Kauai for the best purpose that I could possibly imagine, to bring a template back to earth that had been missing for 2,000 years.

∞ **15** ∞

Montauk

When I first came to Long Island, New York, in May of 1993, I knew nothing of the various experiments that had gone on at the increasingly notorious Montauk radar station, formerly known as Fort Hero, and supposedly abandoned years ago. Shirley Holly, my student of three months, and I, had traveled there because a former client named Danise who lived in the area, had helped us to set up one of the three-day workshops that I gave around the country, and increasingly around the world.

Unbeknownst to me, Shirley had been told by her Higher Self that there were lost souls around Montauk who she could help. I agreed to come along to hold a space for whatever she felt she had to do, and so one night after we finished with our lectures and our clients, we left our respective lodgings and drove out to the Montauk lighthouse, three hours away.

The lost souls that Shirley was thinking of were the island's Native American population, most of whom were extirpated by white settlers and smallpox, as well as the 126 victims of the Spanish-American civil war who died of yellow fever at the island's Camp Wikoff in the 1890's.

She also had in mind all the uncounted sailors who perished with a "mouthful of sand" in the pounding surf under the roving compassionless eye of the Montauk Point lighthouse.

I had seen six clients on the day that Shirley had chosen to visit the lighthouse, and by the time we rolled into the deserted parking lot it was close to 1:00 a.m. The lighthouse, built in 1790, had been completely automated for years. A light fog had rolled in off of the heaving shoulders of the Atlantic, and I could hear the mournful bleating of a fog horn like a lost sheep somewhere out in the void beyond the reach of the probing searchlight high above us. It was about as foreboding a place that I can imagine physically visiting. Before I had time to have second thoughts, Shirley had already bolted the car, intent on her mission. She had reconnoitered the area at sunrise, three days earlier and, unlike me, knew the lay of the land.

I bailed out after her and took up a station behind her, on a rock embankment in front of the lighthouse. I had found over the years that the key to learning about a place was to simply become a part of it, and on this particular occasion I decided to be the lighthouse. Shirley sat down on a narrow strip of sand about thirty feet away from me. As I held my arms out from my sides, turning back and forth in time with the lighthouse, I relaxed, emptied my mind and concentrated only on holding a space for Shirley's work.

I slipped further and further into being the lighthouse, perfectly matching my physical movements to the sweep of the lighthouse beam, and admiring the way the light sparkled off the drops of water that the fog held suspended in the air. Something's here, I thought to myself. I turned with the searchlight and saw something out of the corner of my eye. Shirley's eyes were fixed upon it. It was a man. He was tall, over 6 feet, wearing a dark navy jacket, dark pants, and the kind of cap that sailors often wear.

I looked down at Shirley, still sweeping my arms back and forth in time with the lighthouse. The man stood between us. My first thought was that he must have been a park ranger, come to tell us that the park was closed, but he wore no uniform. There had been no cars, no headlights, nothing to presage his appearance at all.

The man was now standing three feet in front of Shirley, staring intently at her. A rock dislodged under my foot and clattered down the embankment I was standing on. Instantly, the figure whirled and saw me for the first time. At the same moment the beam of the lighthouse swung directly behind me, silhouetting me and illuminating him.

We stared at each other for a long moment that seemed to last for an eternity. I could sense that suddenly becoming aware of me had unnerved him. Shirley sat on the ground behind him, her pale face tilted up toward us as she observed our silent, eerie confrontation. Then, just as suddenly as he had appeared, the mysterious stranger spun on his heel and walked away. A steep cliff rose up like a wall behind Shirley. The man walked straight into the cliff and disappeared. I stared after him, all of the hairs on my neck standing on end. He had vanished without a trace.

It was a little harder to be a lighthouse after that. Nevertheless, I continued my slow sweeps until Shirley had finished her releasement process, which took about five minutes. We linked up on the path back up to the car, the ocean and the shore hissing reproachfully behind us.

Both of us had seen exactly the same thing. The enigmatic dark figure had simply dematerialized, like he had walked through an invisible door. "Let's follow him," Shirley whispered. I shot her an incredulous look and shook my head, firmly. There was no way that I was going to follow some military phantom who could appear and disappear at will. My unconscious mind had other ideas. Part of me went ahead and followed him anyway. The same thing happened to Shirley. The end result was that a fragment of each of us would remain marooned at some kind of interdimensional military base on Mars until we retrieved them during a session two years later.

We conferred further back at the car, with the engine running and the doors locked. The figure that we had both seen was identical. We both had heard footsteps which meant that he was physically present. Whoever or whatever he was, we theorized, he was probably drawn to us by Shirley's intent and purpose. Since I had no intent, he hadn't seen me until my concern for Shirley made me visible again. Two years later, in 1995, we would work with a Montauk "survivor" who would tell us that the lighthouse was regularly patrolled by members of something he called "Delta Force" and that we had been lucky to escape with our lives. At the time we didn't know that we had just had a narrow scrape. It was simply surreal.

By then it was close to 2:00 a.m. in the morning and I was ready for bed. Shirley, disappointed that we hadn't followed the curious phantom, had other ideas. She pointed out that the gate to the Montauk radar station was on our way home, and only five minutes away from the lighthouse. I sighed. Instead of going back to the safety of the warm beds that awaited each of us, we drove to the gate of the Montauk radar station, where Shirley felt she had more work to do. I listened incredulously as she breathlessly told me her plan. She was going to sneak through a hole in the six foot metal fence around the facility to inspect the base itself. I looked around at the dark somber buildings, the radar antenna against the sky like a black spider web, and all of the signs that said:

175

"Absolutely No Admittance." I looked back at Shirley in disbelief, as she eyed the base with a reckless gleam in her eyes.

"Are you crazy?" I sputtered. My counterproposal was that we use the main gate to access the memories of the place, rather than risk our necks poking around an abandoned military installation in the dark. Reluctantly, she agreed to my plan.

I waded through the tall dry grass, wrapped my fingers around the chain-link fence and moved into the silence. Very quickly the fence melted away, to be replaced by alternating patterns of white and dark swirling energy. My body fell away. I was inside some type of vortex or tunnel. Almost as soon as I knew this, I felt the opening to the tunnel closing behind me like the mouth of a snake. It was a trap, like the forty foot deep pits that rotted trees left in sand dunes. They called them devil's sinkholes. I had blundered blindly into the multidimensional equivalent.

I shifted my intent to keeping the door of the tunnel open. As soon as I held that focus, I felt a powerful surge of potential energy, as if a bolt of lightning was about to strike and then thousands of souls rose upwards, passing me like a huge flock of migrating birds. I glimpsed men in black military uniforms and combat fatigues, some in long-sleeved blue jumpsuits and many children, mostly boys. The children were naked, and very frightened. I also saw thin, frail alien life forms, far less of them than there were humans. They had huge oversized eyes without pupils. As the last of this strange parade of beings flew past me, their collective pain, fear and suffering washed over me like the wake of a freighter over a dugout canoe.

Flashes of everything that had ever happened on the base flickered through my awareness like I was a VCR running at one hundred times normal speed. I saw trucks coming and going under cover of night, rooms full of glowing electronic equipment, miles of underground tunnels, chicken wire compartments where children were kenneled like dogs, a buried spaceship, and men in lab coats bending over pale white bodies. I knew that some of the worst things that I could possibly imagine had happened here. I also felt an unidentified presence lurking nearby, something with a vibration that I had never felt before.

The energy flowing past me diminished and then stopped. I felt a profound sense of relief, as if the base itself had been waiting for this moment. I moved carefully out of the tunnel and mentally sealed up the entrance so that no one would ever be trapped there again. As soon as I finished I was lost in an endless dark void. There was no direction, no up or down, no way home at all. I called out to Shirley, barely able to hear the sound of my own voice.

Now it was Shirley's turn to become the lighthouse. Like a lost ship, I turned and steamed blindly through the darkness toward her, feeling the love that I had asked her to send me grow stronger and stronger until I came back to the time and place where both she and my physical body waited.

I felt the gradual return of the cold steel wire against my fingers as I found my way back to conscious awareness of my surroundings. I sagged against the fence while I recovered my bearings. I'd never seen anything like that tunnel before, and had no idea why I'd find such a thing at an abandoned radar base.

I shuffled around to see Shirley staring at me with a mixture of perplexed amusement and concern. I had disappeared just like the mysterious man at the beach had. She had seen my body become fuzzy and indistinct, and then it became just a bright pink outline like a neon sign, and then she saw nothing at all. Cool, I thought to myself. I'd wanted to be invisible since I was in the first grade.

By then Shirley and I both knew that there was definitely something very out of the ordinary about Montauk, Long Island, although we lacked the information we needed to put the pieces together. Our ignorance was a kind of a blessing, because it allowed us to learn things experientially that our conscious minds would otherwise have had a very hard time accepting.

The ball of yarn continued to unravel. The next day, only a day before we were to leave Long Island, I received a call from an extremely reticent individual who was interested in making an appointment with me for a friend that he was very concerned about. Fortunately, or by design, I had space for one more appointment before I was scheduled to return to Texas. Later that same day I had my first encounter with the beings I call "the watchers."

I had just stepped out of the building where we held our lectures to eat my lunch on the steps. Immediately, I had the uncomfortable feeling that I was being stared at. My observer sat motionless on the tailgate of a delivery truck, eyeing me from across the parking lot like a cat. I stared back and met nothing in return. His eyes were like the windows of an abandoned house, completely vacant. Even though they tracked my every move, I could not detect any of the energies that I normally associate with personality. He was as empty as the husk a cicada leaves behind when it molts, a human video camera, observing without thought or emotion. His perceptions were relayed elsewhere. I've seen many other watchers since, but only when I've been on business in some way connected with the Montauk project or one of its many offshoots.

The following day, my last on Long Island, the mysterious friend of a friend finally came to see me. He was shy,

178

extremely polite, absolutely honest and had a curious ageless quality about him, as though he were somehow simultaneously both child and adult.

I'd never in my life seen anyone whose life fields were in such disarray. His emotional body was literally fifty feet out, almost completely divorced from his physical body. This helped to explain what he had told me in his interview, that he felt completely out of touch with his emotions, and had no understanding of them. From a psychic point of view, he was about as out of touch as you could possibly be and still be alive. I had never seen a case like his before. He also brought documents from a neurologist, which basically said that the only functioning part of his brain was his brainstem, the oldest part of the brain, mainly thought to be responsible for basic functions like respiration. He thought that this had happened to him because he had been the principal psychic in the Montauk experiments. Our immediate task was to retrieve his emotional body. Neither Shirley nor I had any idea of how to proceed.

The universe, it's said, never gives you a challenge that you can't handle. Proceeding on this assumption, I directed my client to pull his emotional body back to a place where he could feel again.

He responded by becoming completely rigid. Then he stopped breathing, and started turning blue.

At first I thought that my instructions had thrown him into some kind of a coma. However, as minutes passed without him so much as twitching an eyelid in response to my repeated entreaties, I began to worry that I had inadvertently put him in a much worse state than a coma. I began to wonder if he was dead.

With each transit of the second hand on my watch, the more bizarre his condition seemed to become. He was as stiff as a freshly milled board, only his head, heels and fingertips touching the massage table. I wondered if perhaps I really was as dangerous as I had once thought. I remembered the nuclear explosion that I had witnessed long ago from my parents' car in Nevada, how it reminded me of my lifetime in Turkey, and how it seemed to say to me that power, all power, was dangerous. I had created so much pain and suffering in my life, and in the lives of others, by struggling against the forces that seemed to dictate that I become a healer. Now the long road that I had traveled seemed to have suddenly and ignominiously ended, leaving me staring in shocked amazement at the cold, and apparently lifeless man on the table in front of me.

Shirley looked at me in shock. I shook my head helplessly. I realized that no matter what I thought I knew, I really knew nothing at all. My client's pallor had worsened. It was time for CPR, and an ambulance.

Then, at that moment when I completely surrendered, and admitted to myself and the universe that I really knew nothing, a miracle happened. Suddenly I knew exactly what to do.

I bent down and whispered: "I am a friend. I have been sent to help you. I am not of this place." The man jerked on the table like he had just been defibrillated. He was alive.

I leaned closer and repeated the words that I was hearing so clearly in my own head: "I have trained for a long time to help you, and I want you to take whatever energy you need to take back control of your body." I placed my hands on his heart. They warmed instantly, and the rest of my body with them, both indicators of the amount of energy that he was pulling through me. His eyelids fluttered slightly and then he nodded almost imperceptibly when I questioned him. He was back.

My client's participation in the experiments at Montauk had both damaged his body's subtle fields and literally burned out parts of his brain. He could not remember what his mind had been like before the experiments began. I thought for a moment about how I could best help him, and the answer that I received was to share the structure of my mind with him, so that he would have a kind of blueprint to begin rebuilding his own. My knowing was the legacy of my experience in Kauai. I leaned over and touched my forehead to his, and allowed him to see exactly what my mental and emotional templates looked like. I would realize years later that this procedure allowed me to know everything that he knew, and thus repaid me many times over for my healing work with the knowledge that he had accumulated through his years of involvement with Montauk.

My client's fields were now stabilized but were still further out than was normal. Was there, I asked him, a shape or a symbol that he could use which would allow his emotional body to come back in safely?

"Yes," he murmured. He described a shape that was something like a teardrop. We used the shape that his Higher Self had given us to bring his emotional body back even closer. I was careful to give him permission to stop at any point, in case he tipped into another coma.

By the end of the session my client seemed vastly improved. He gave me a book about Montauk to read. Inside the book, I found a drawing of a being Preston Nichols, one of the authors of the book, had dubbed "Junior." Junior was a flesh and blood monster, created in much the same way as the fictional monster in the fifties science fiction movie, *Forbidden Planet*.

My client had been part of the Montauk project since his birth in the 1950's. Prior to that, he had been a senior engineer on the USS Eldridge, in charge of the generators that provided the power for the Philadelphia Experiment. How he was able to be on board the Eldridge in 1943 and then be born a decade later is a subject beyond the scope of this book, but is covered elsewhere. He had a unique ability to focus and hold a point in the time space continuum, which allowed the physical creation of a vortex. It was this vortex that allowed the experimenters at the Montauk base to build upon earlier experiments and physically send people through time and space.

Many of the people that were sent through the tunnel were homeless men and women, and runaway children. The base's proximity to New York city afforded the researchers an almost unlimited supply of experimental subjects. According to several sources, large numbers of these unfortunate people were either lost in time or psychically traumatized.

The Montauk experiments did not begin nor end with just time travel. They also encompassed research into mind control using ELF waves, kundalini energy, and direct physical manifestation. The mind control experiments were perhaps the most chilling of all of the various otherwordly manipulations that were carried out there. Survivors of Montauk report that many of the mind control experiments were carried out on young children. These children, known as the Montauk Boys were confined in kennels, deep inside a cement bunker. These kennels and the bunker have been extensively videotaped as recently as 1993. The experimenters were most interested in being able to recreate fear, and many of these children were literally scared to death in the process.

My client, like any human being, felt immense guilt over his involvement with these experiments. Consequently, he conspired with Preston Nichols, one of the base's engineers, to create a monster that would destroy the project, hopefully, for all time. This was Junior, whose picture I had seen in the book.

Within two days of my session with my client, I found myself getting progressively sicker. I felt dizzy, disoriented and nauseous. When it kept getting worse I sat down to meditate and I found that my emotional fields were wobbling and out of balance. There was a dark angry presence within them. It was confused, angry, and hurt. It was also nearly fifteen feet tall, and was covered with thick black fur like a Yeti, the spitting image of the picture that I'd seen in my client's Montauk book. I had picked up a fragment of Junior.

Junior, as it turned out, consisted of little else but the intent to destroy the Montauk radar station. With me, Junior had no purpose whatsoever and he wanted desperately to change form and become something useful again. I was happy to oblige and felt much more useful myself after he left.

I found out much more about Montauk over the next two years, both from seeing other survivors as clients, and from the increasingly numerous books, videos, and cassettes on the subject that they brought with them. Most of the living participants had been subjected to a careful electronic brainwashing, very similar to that reportedly suffered by victims of UFO abductions. The memories were carefully hidden behind the participant's worse fears, something the experimenters knew a great deal about. Inevitably, these memories slowly returned, like the bodies of murder victims that defied weights and chains to eventually surface. Preston Nichols, the engineer who was the very first to go public with his memories, experienced their return while tinkering with a radio antenna on his roof during a thunderstorm. Gradually the survivors of

Montauk sought each other out, corroborating each other's stories, helping each other to heal, and convincing each other that the terrible nightmares and waking visions that they had seen, were in fact real.

Montauk's detractors say the same kinds of things about the project, and about the Philadelphia experiment, that have been said to UFO researchers and abduction victims for decades, mainly that their stories were the working of a kind of collective hysteria. I don't believe this for an instant. I've held the victims and empathically experienced what they went through and I've psychically accessed the memories held by the base itself. The real question that Montauk brings to us is not was it real, but whether we can face the darkest reflections of ourselves without flinching. At Montauk, at Auschwitz, at Sand Creek, or in the former Yugoslavia, these questions are always the same. The day is coming when we will no longer need to ask them.

Montauk continued to be part of my life after I left Long Island. In fact, in my next workshop, in Buffalo, my first client walked in with a copy of the same book that I had seen the picture of Junior in. I soon found that the victims of Montauk would find me no matter where I was.

The following year, in 1994 I held my first seven day practitioner training in Austin, Texas. It was such a success that we immediately planned to hold another one in 1995, and we chose Long Island as the location. Shirley and I both felt that because of what had happened in the area, we would have no difficulty finding interesting clients for our in-class demonstrations. Sure enough, by the time of the workshop, several more survivors of Montauk came forward, including members of a kind of interdimensional special forces group similar to that portrayed in the movie *Stargate*. They referred to their

184

unit as the Delta Force, which curiously enough is also the name of an elite army helicopter unit.

The Delta Force team members that we saw told riveting stories about being abducted as boys, secretly transported to the base in windowless trucks, and then being led down long hospital corridors by men in white coats. At the ends of the corridors were rooms with stainless steel tables in them. The boys were stripped naked, strapped to the tables and some type of apparatus was attached to their genitals. They were then subject to a highly refined version of Wilhelm Reich's orgone technology, which was used to cycle their sexual energy in a continuous loop until it increased by a factor of fifty. At that point the energy forced its way through a small opening at the top of the spine into the oldest part of the brain, and it became possible for the carefully programmed victims to become physically manifest at any point in time that their handlers could provide them a "witness" for. A witness is any object that possesses the vibration of a particular time, such as a roman talent from the time of the crucifixion. Both the technique of traveling through time via the agency of a witness, and the looping of sexual energy were well known within ancient mystery schools, and to the shamans of indigenous cultures. The difference was that until Montauk, these practices could take a lifetime of discipline and spiritual preparation to master while the methods used at Montauk worked almost immediately.

One of our Montauk clients reported waking up from a nightmare to find himself covered with blood and the floor strewn with strange metallic objects, the likes of which he had never seen before. Apparently, he had woken up in the middle of an implant procedure. He intended to bring the objects to our workshop to show our

185

students, only to have all of them disappear under mysterious circumstances the night before his presentation.

Another of the Delta Force Team members that I worked on had an etheric implant in the form of a thin wire laid into his spine. It functioned as a kind of leash, the purpose of which was to prevent him from being able to travel through time on his own or attack his overseers. It worked just like a surge arrestor protects a computer. When my client's kundalini energy reached a certain potential, the implant vented the excess energy out of the small of his back, thus rendering him powerless. As soon as I removed his implant, using psychic surgery, I felt a sharp pain. I was left with a bright red circular burn about an inch in diameter in the center of my back. It took several months to finally heal.

After his session, I realized that I now had enough information to attempt the project of time travel myself. I told the class what I was doing, and I had Shirley hold a space for me while I began cycling my kundalini energy around my body, consciously raising its intensity until I had increased it by a factor of fifty. At that moment, I felt it surge into the back of my head, and then, as has happened many other times in my life, everything changed.

I was in a brilliant white void, the oldest void of all, surrounded by an infinite number of floating black specks. Each speck was a timeline, leading to a different event. Unfortunately, none of them were labeled. They had to be chosen by intuition. It was the interdimensional version of the old carnival string game. I gazed at the sea of floating black dots for a long moment, and then I chose.

Once again I was back at the crucifixion, staring up at Jesus on the cross. Contrary to what I'd heard about the green hills of Cavalry, the site of the crucifixion that I visited was one of the most awful places imaginable, a stinking rat-infested garbage dump. The crosses were only slightly taller than the victims who languished upon them, so that many of those crucified had their eyes gouged out by vultures or their feet chewed to the bones by rats while they were still alive.

I moved further backwards in time, to be with Jesus again, but at a place where His vibration and His intent were absolutely pure. I found myself in the desert with Him, witnessing something that appeared to be very much like a Native American vision quest. He was twenty six years old and about to embark upon His life's mission. I was thus privileged to feel His essence in as pure a form as it ever had been on earth, before His vibration became altered and distorted by history, and by the projections of those around Him. His essence when I saw Him at that time was also thus the purest possible reflection of ourselves. He was like the tuning fork, a reference being for all of us.

The distortion of this pure vibration as it echoed through time, left us with an imperfect recording of Christ's true essence. This recording, while it may have been perfectly appropriate to our evolution a thousand years ago, or even yesterday, may not best serve us where we are now. I believe that it was this altered memory of the original vibration of Christ, together with our longing for His return, that allowed the rise and fall of many powerful figures throughout our recorded history.

The perfection that I was able to empathically experience at that moment is almost impossible to imagine, let alone describe. Absolute compassion—even at the moment of His death, unconditional love, total absence of judgment, humility, and an overwhelming gentleness, all welled forth from Him like sweet water from a beautiful spring in that desolate place. I fully understood, for

187

the first time, that the key to Christ's boundless compassion for others was that He first had absolute compassion for Himself.

Christ's energy also felt strongly feminine in nature, and here I mean feminine only in the sense that we understand it at this moment in time. More precisely, Christ's vibration was a reflection of what it meant to be truly male. He had an inexhaustible gentleness, a state of being that somewhere along the way, we had come to mistakenly associate only with the feminine.

I also saw the gateway that Christ used to return to Source when He left his body. Its symbol is a cross within a circle, which corresponded to the movement He made, literally spinning out of His body to return to Abba, His father. This symbol has since become very important to me. It is the symbol that I share with my students so that they can access the gentle Christ being within each of them.

I opened my eyes to see my student's expectant faces. How could I explain what I had just seen? I realized that I didn't need to explain anything. I could let them feel what I had felt for themselves, as best they were able. Then they would know.

I could still feel the Christ vibration resonating within me like a plucked violin string. I focused on it, amplifying it, sending it out so that everyone around me could experience it as well. Each of the students in the room, as they came to know the undistorted vibration of Christ, would in turn be able to share it with others. "This," I told them, "is what it feels like. This is how you will know it."

As soon as I spoke those words, I remembered hearing them years ago in a temple on Kauai. Then the old Hindu priest had been talking about me to his students, and now here I was in front of my own students using the same words to describe Jesus. Everything was a circle. All of the

188

times that I had been able to bridge different realities were exercises designed to prepare me for this moment, and this moment was an exercise designed to prepare me for something else. Every moment of my life had trained me for every other moment. Everything had purpose. Everything was exactly as it should be.

Ken Page can be reached at:

INSTITUTE OF MULTIDIMENSIONAL
CELLULAR HEALING ™
901B Hwy 80, Suite 222
San Marcos, Texas 78666-8115 USA
Ph/fax: (512) 376-3336

Please contact the Institute for information on
upcoming special events, private and remote phone
sessions, weekend workshops, and Practitioner Training
classes. We will be glad to answer your questions and send
you information as well as a free audio tape of Ken
discussing his work, philosophies and MCH™.

Available from the Institute:

BOOKS

The Traveler Ken Page And The Fallen Angel
Throughout history men, like King Arthur, have searched
for the Holy Grail, wondering if the legend could be true
and the Holy Grail is only waiting for rediscovery. Join
Ken as he unravels one of the oldest secrets known to
mankind, along with Daniel, his son from a past life.

    ISBN 0-9649703-0-9 $11.95

The Traveler: Man's Search for Soul
This book goes into great detail about cellular imprints,
emotional signatures, symbols, polarities, entity interference, thoughtforms, lost souls, health issues, karmic,

emotional and traumatic links to past lives, recognizing psychic attack, space connections, walk-ins, and clearing multidimensional blocks. Transcripts from client sessions which demonstrate Ken's healing process and its application in specific issues are included.

ISBN 0-9649703-2-5 $11.95

The Traveler And The End Of Time
The Secret Life of Ken Page
Contains dozens of fascinating and inspiring true stories, from the life of Ken Page. Starting with his humble beginnings as a seven year old entrepreneur, through his years as a millionaire businessman, to a dramatic series of miracles, triumphs, and tragedies that permitted him to do nothing else but what he is today: an internationally famous facilitator of healing.

ISBN 0-9649703-1-7 $11.95

MCH™ Philosophies and Applications
Basic Instruction Manual. Prerequisite to MCH™ 9-day Practitioner Training. $30.00

Advanced MCH™ Techniques
Advanced Instruction Manual for MCH™ 9-day Practitioner Training. $30.00

For the Love of August Blue - a novel
August Blue tells the story about an eccentric old man who believes that his mission on earth is to bring God to justice. On the way he becomes a national celebrity and effects the lives of all around them. Available in 1996

VIDEOS

Christ Consciousness Breathing Techniques,
  The Living Light Breath™ Video and Instructions
Two thousand years ago, a gate or portal was created and opened to all human consciousness by the Being known as Jesus of Nazareth, or Christ. The gate, which connects the body and the spirit, the realms above and the realms below, and the inner worlds with the outer worlds, was created and opened at the time of His death. The gate was specifically activated as Christ took His last physical breath, and moved into the Living Light Breath™. The Living Light Breath™ is a way to move into unity consciousness. $19.95

The Animal Healing and Clearing Video
Learn how to fully experience nature as well as how to clear and balance animals and pets. $19.95

An Introduction to Ken Page and Multidimensional
  Cellular Healing™ 1/2 hr. $5.95

AUDIO TAPES

An Introduction to Ken Page and Multidimensional
  Cellular Healing™
Ken discussing his work, philosophies and MCH™. free

Holographic Healing Tones and Sacred Sounds
A 30-minute tape of Ken Page using sound to shift and clear cellular imprints. $9.95

PRIVATE AND REMOTE PHONE SESSIONS

MCH™ is a way to discover your own self truth. Its purpose is to assist you by integrating your whole being with your Higher Self. MCH™ looks for patterns that your subconscious mind is giving energy. Often times, no matter how much work we may have done to understand our mental, emotional, spiritual, and physical issues, there seems to be a missing piece which blocks our final resolution of these problems. As a result, we create patterns, over and over in our life, so that we may have yet another chance to gain the wisdom, understanding, and knowledge of our lessons. In addition, any fears or emotional residue we may be holding over a particular issue may throw further illusion over the problem, making it almost impossible to see "the bigger picture". MCH™ addresses ways the inner mind can assist in breaking through these self-made and limiting barriers.

MCH™ WORKSHOPS

THE TRAVELER AND THE
LIVING LIGHT LOOP

A 12-hour program. All participants will be shown how to be centered and move into creatorship as well as full body awareness and beingness. Learn how to experience each moment throughout every cell in the body. Also taught will be the Living Light Breath™, which will allow you to bring Ascension into the personal experience of 'Inscension' as well as access higher dimensions. Some of the things you may experience in the workshop are:
• Learn how to stay in your space energetically, and have

more energy • Find out why things are going faster, and find quietness and calmness within that accelerated flow. • Learn Bi-Location Techniques • Learn Holographic Healing and Rejuvenation • Explore your mission and purpose for being on the planet at this time • Find out how to really be in the moment, instead of the past or the future • Discover a new way to lucid dream, and work out issues in the dream state • How to be in balance with both your inner male and female aspects • Find out how to dialogue in writing with your Higher Self, and get answers that you can trust • Learn how to connect with the dolphin and whale consciousness, and use it in your healing work • Get symbols that will help you to connect with information from your past, and from other realities • Receive three valuable and unique holograms that contain special information, both energetically, and visually • Learn to access a sacred, energetic gate created over 2,000 years ago • Have a chance to participate in a group-session with Ken, and understand what you have created in your past.

SHAMANISTIC HEALING
AND ANIMAL CLEARING

A 4-hour program in which all participants will be shown how to fully experience nature, as well as how to clear and balance their own animals or pets. Live horses, cats and dogs will be used in the class demonstrations.

THE MCH™ PRACTITIONER TRAINING

A NINE day, 80-hour experiential training that extensively expands the concepts and techniques of Multi-dimensional Cellular Healing™ to include the very latest knowledge and information. Students will observe complete client sessions, highlighting the latest MCH™

techniques. They will also have the opportunity to practice sessions of their own.

Topics covered in detail in the course may be, and are not limited to:

Psychic surgery
Dual regressions
Group regressions
Induction techniques
In-Utero Regressions
Rebirthing techniques
Holographic picturing
Addictions and phobias
Self clearing techniques
Unusual toning techniques
Remote session techniques
ET interference and implants
Drug, alcohol, and food abuse
Dehaunting of physical locations
Working with children and animals
Witchcraft, voodoo, curses and spells
Reconnection to place of personal origin
Handling of the ego, will, and client blocks
Recovery of oversoul fragments, soul theft, breakaways

Also included will be several different forms of Holographic Mind-Body Integration techniques which may be whole body breathing, Tai-Chi, Yoga, using the breath to travel, projecting 3D into other dimensions, and expanding empathic abilities.

Certification involves completion of MCH™ Practitioner Course, workbooks, and submission of video taped client sessions which demonstrate the participant's knowledge and expertise. Upon approval by staff members of completed course materials, students may reference themselves as an MCH™ Practitioner.